# ALL ABOUT CHILDREN
## QUESTIONS PARENTS ASK

Tony Humphreys

Newleaf

Newleaf
an imprint of
Gill & Macmillan Ltd
Hume Avenue, Park West
Dublin 12
with associated companies throughout the world
www.gillmacmillan.ie

© Tony Humphreys 2004
0 7171 3740 6

Index compiled by Gráinne Farren
Print origination by Carrigboy Typesetting Services, Co. Cork
Printed by ColourBooks Ltd, Dublin

*The paper used in this book comes from the wood pulp of managed forests. For every tree felled, at least one tree is planted, thereby renewing natural resources.*

This book is typeset in 11.5pt on 15pt AfgaRotisSemisans.

A catalogue record for this book is available from the British Library.

5   4   3

*Books by the same author*
A Different Kind of Teacher
The Power of 'Negative' Thinking
Self-Esteem: The Key to Your Child's Future
Myself, My Partner
A Different Kind of Discipline
Work and Worth: Take Back Your Life
Examining Our Times
Whose Life Are You Living?
Leaving the Nest: What Families Are All About

*Audio tapes and CDs by the same author*
Self-Esteem for Adults
Raising Your Child's Self-Esteem
Work and Self

# CONTENTS

# INTRODUCTION

So many parents have said to me over the years that if they had any idea of what parenting really involved, they probably would not have chosen to have children. Sadly, these are parents who have honestly expressed that they were sorry they ever had children! And there are a high percentage of parents, who, while admitting the daunting challenges that rearing children brings, would do it all over again. What is certain is that the cuddly baby fantasy can quickly be extinguished by the sometimes exhausting and frustrating experiences of caring for children.

The differences in the above responses to having a family can be due to several circumstances, not least the fact that each parent, whether aware of it or not, brings his or her emotional baggage into the role of family architect. The level of personal vulnerability is often a good index of the level of parental effectiveness. It is still a fact that mothers do 90 per cent of the parenting, in spite of the fact that most mothers also work outside the home. The unprecedented rise in single parenting and the sad fact that many marriages break down within seven years are other factors that add to the stress of parenting.

To gift life to a child is a wonderful and unselfish action on behalf of a parent. The challenge arises in the maintaining of that unselfishness and the provision of a dynamic and positive home environment for the child's realisation of self. In creating the latter, parents need to be mindful that all parenting starts with self (see Chapter One) and that attention to their own self-realisation cannot be interrupted by the responsibilities of parenthood. Managing these two relationships — with child and with self — and, where there is a two-parent family, keeping sight of the couple relationship, are sizeable tasks. Parents ask many questions on these key relationships, and Chapters One and Two present the most frequently asked questions. Other areas of concern are career, the role of fathers and the influence of grandparents.

Parenting is not an instinctual activity but rather a profession that requires each parent to understand self, to develop parenting skills, to respond constructively to the many challenging behaviours that children present and to learn from their own challenging behaviours so that their vulnerabilities do not block the emergence of the child's sense of self. Not easy tasks, but these are skills that each parent has the endless potential to develop. Parents need all the help they can get, but ultimately they need to rely on their own wisdom, intuition, knowledge and skill. Parents need to continue to update their knowledge and skills, not only because society continues to radically change, but because the needs of and the challenges that children pose change as they grow up. There now seems to be a dawning recognition by governments that parenting is the most important profession of all, and training programmes and parent coaching are beginning to be made available to parents. To date, services have focused on crisis situations rather than prevention through the education of parents for their key role in society. There is also a developing realisation among work organisations that being person/marriage/family-friendly makes for a more contented and productive work environment.

Chapter Three focuses on essential parenting skills, while Chapters Four and Five deal with ways to effectively understand and respond to children's and parents' own challenging behaviours. It is in these three areas that most questions arise, particularly in the area of the difficult behaviours children may show. Parents have not been strongly supported to tackle their own challenging actions, which, inevitably, pose a threat to children's welfare; and yet parents are unlikely to be effective in coping with children's challenging behaviours when they are not effectively dealing with their own.

All parents are concerned with the educational and future welfare of their children and this concern is reflected in the number of parents who seek help from me and my colleagues on the educational progress of their children. The issues that arise around children's education and future can be seen in the questions posed in Chapter Six. Parents are the primary educators and it is they, along with teachers, who need to ensure that learning is an adventure for children. However, once again, if learning and work are sources of threat for parents, they cannot be in a position to inspire their children. Parents and teachers have a responsibility to free themselves of their fears around learning so that they become sound and solid educators of their children.

It is because of the courage of those parents and children who have sought help for their difficulties that this book has been made possible. In the course of the twenty-five years that I have been helping families, there are few difficulties that I have not encountered, and the practises recommended here have been well and truly tested.

This book is meant to be a practical handbook for parents and is set out in a way that I hope is user-friendly. I would encourage prospective parents to read the book, if only to understand that parenting starts with self.

# CHAPTER ONE

# WHERE DOES PARENTING BEGIN?

## INTRODUCTION

All parenting begins with self. The nature of each parent's relationship with self will determine how they relate to each child. I deliberately say *each* child because *each child has a different parent*. This has to be the case, as the parent is unique and has fashioned responses to her experiences in a way that manifests that individuality. Equally, the child is unique and will do likewise. Therefore, when two individuals interact it is always a unique experience – hence each child has a different parent! The parent who protests that 'I treat all the children the same' will pile up problems for herself and her offspring, as she is neither in touch with her own uniqueness nor that of her child. There is nothing surer than the reality that each child has a fierce determination to express his or her individuality, and it takes very powerful blocking experiences to dilute or extinguish the light of a child's uniqueness. It is the wise parent who, acting out from her own solid place of unique interiority, affirms and supports all efforts on the child's part to establish his or her individual presence in the family.

A major responsibility for parents who, because of their earlier experiences in their family of origin, may have had to hide many aspects of their self, is to recover what is hidden. The more a parent brings the fullness of who she is to her relationship with her child, the more the child will hold onto his or her own fullness. It is a truism that a parent can only bring her child to the same level of maturation that she has realised herself. This is why it is incumbent on each parent to parent self, because any neglect of self will manifest itself in some way or other in the parenting of children.

Parenting is the core profession in society, and training and preparation for the parenting of children is essential. Parenting is not an instinctual behaviour, but rather a highly sophisticated and complex repertoire of skills. Parents have responsibility for the physical, emotional, social, sexual, behavioural, educational, creative and spiritual development of children. Most of all, they have the responsibility of loving children unconditionally. On this issue, there can be no benign neglect, as unconditional love is the *sine qua non* of effective parenting. However, a parent cannot love unconditionally if she first has not learned to love herself. So many parents ask me, 'How do I parent myself?' (see Question 3 below). The fact that they ask the question indicates an urgent need to reflect on their own childhood experiences and how that has influenced the way in which they currently relate to self. In working with families over many years I have found that I can trace the origins of the presenting difficulties back at least five generations. This phenomenon has nothing to do with genes, but it has got to do with unresolved conflicts and emotional baggage being passed from generation to generation. Unless parents reflect on their experiences and take the actions needed to free themselves from their fears and insecurities, the darkness of immaturity will perpetuate. All too often, the unconscious defences of 'it's in the genes' or 'it's in their nature' or 'it's his or her personality type' have been employed by parents so that they do not have to face their own insecurities. Parents need all the help and support they can get to resolve their inner pain and realise their uniqueness and fullness. It is in the understanding and realising of self that parents create the readiness for the responsibility of rearing children.

The first four questions in the chapter focus on the nature of the self, the fact that some parents feel guilty about taking time for self, how a parent can best maintain a sense of self, and the fact that how a parent feels about self affects her parenting of children. Relationship issues of controlling, boundaries, 'emotional intelligence' and anger management are broached in Questions 5 to 8. The final question focuses on how best to prepare for parenting.

## Q1.  WHAT DO YOU MEAN BY THE SELF?

I read recently that the notion of self, self-esteem or self-worth is a post-industrial phenomenon that has come about because wealth has provided opportunities for reflection and the indulgence of ideas of the self.

Clearly, the author of this stance has not read Socrates who, thousands of years ago, encouraged people to 'know thyself'. Christ preached 'love self' and Buddha encouraged people 'to nourish your true self'. There are earlier texts in India (at least 6000 years old) that talk about the primacy of self. In these texts the author proclaims that in all relationships 'it is the Self that should be seen, the Self that should be heard, the Self that should be reflected upon, and the Self that should be known'.

The self of each person is at the heart of everything that a person does, says, thinks, feels and dreams. It is not that the idea of 'the self' is a new concept, but it is a belief that comes and goes depending on the level of maturity of cultures. In major social systems (family, community, school, workplace) where the sacredness and individuality of each member is not affirmed, the individual person has to hide who he or she really is and conform to the conditional demands of the social system. Conditionality is a way of relating which values certain behaviours and loses sight of the immense worth of the person. Not surprisingly, a preoccupation with what other people think, or with work or success, is common, as individuals feel their value lies in what they do and not in their unique presence. Ironically, when behaviour becomes more important than the self, then learning, creativity, responsibility and productivity are greatly reduced and everybody loses out. The self is unique, sacred, immutable, capable, gifted, lovable, expansive, intuitive, imaginative and inspirational. Many of these self qualities are blocked when behaviour becomes the yardstick of a person's worth.

In any social situation it is vital that adults guard against anonymity. Parents and teachers need to ensure that the presence and absence of each individual matters. There is nothing more devastating to a person than for a particular behaviour to be singled out as a reason for either rejection or affirmation. It is not often appreciated that the child or adult who is told 'you're brilliant' because of high academic or work performance is more at risk than the child or adult who is told 'you're a fool' because of some failure experience. The individual labelled 'brilliant' conforms to the pressure to continue this behaviour, but the major pressure and strain is to hide his or her real self.

It is estimated that anywhere between 20 and 25 per cent of young people experience depression. In my clinical experience, depression in young people is the manifestation of having to depress who they really are. Similarly, those young and, indeed, older people who suffer high anxiety, are manifesting their fear or terror of showing who they really are. Think about how hard it is to be real in the face of a parent or teacher or boss who rigidly and aggressively wants you to conform to his or her ways. The more intense the demands, the greater the fear of being oneself. There are many students who are under considerable pressure and stress, but the pressure they exert on themselves is to hide who they really are. On the surface, the pressure would appear to be caused by examinations and career demands, but the deeper issue concerns the self.

Adults have a responsibility to free themselves of the shackles of conditionality and to liberate the self. When adults free themselves of their fears by expressing the fullness and breadth of their unique selves, their presence will offer opportunities for others, especially their children, to liberate their unique selves. Adults can only bring children to the same level of expression of self that they have reached themselves. This is also true for teachers, doctors, healthcare professionals, political leaders and organisational heads.

There are some who may defensively reject the above as being spiritually based, but I believe that love of self and others is essential, practical and expedient if we are to live in harmony with each other. The challenge is there for all, no one excepted.

## Q2. ISN'T TAKING TIME FOR SELF A SELFISH ACTIVITY?

It is amazing the number of people who still hold on to the belief that love of self is an act of selfishness. These people also believe that individuality is the cause of the breakdown of marital and family relationships. Maybe they are confusing individuality with individualism. Individuality is about the expression of your real and authentic self. The words of Shakespeare extol the soundness of being true to your unique self: 'To thine own self be true, and as sure as night follows day thou canst not then be false to any man.'

Individualism, on the other hand, is a narcissism that springs from the desert of a loveless interiority and attempts to compel and manipulate others into being there for you. This is the face of dependence, possessiveness, control, aggression, jealousy, attention-seeking, rigidity and violence. There is another form of individualism, which is less obvious, but just as insidious. This is the attainment of recognition by wanting others to always need you, and any attempt by them to become independent will be greeted with withdrawal, hostile silences, sulking and rejection.

Love is absolutely vital for human life. You cannot love another person unless you are equally involved in the difficult but wondrous work of learning to love yourself. The extent of your own regard for yourself will be the measure of your relationships with others. Parents can only love their children to the same level that they love themselves. Therapists can only bring clients to the same level of development that they themselves have attained. Leaders are only effective to the extent they have charge of their own selves. Authority means authorship of self, not of others.

The task of loving self is difficult, not because we do not possess amazing power to change, but because the majority of people have learned cleverly to conform to the fashioning of a persona to meet the expectations of others. To do otherwise would have meant risking further darkening of their presence. People who are dependent on others subconsciously know full well the implications of expressing their true selves. They also know that these dangers will exist for their children if they are encouraged through love to express their individuality and power beyond measure. They risk exposing themselves to hostility, ridicule, labelling, criticism, aggression, manipulation and violence. Staying hidden behind the defensive walls of conformity does bring a certain comfort, but what a shame that progress is blocked towards finding your own true self and giving children permission to be free to be themselves.

A groundswell whereby many people make the journey inwards is needed to lighten the task – the duty to love self and the duty to love others. It has to be seen that these duties go hand in hand and both processes need to be encouraged, supported and celebrated. The Catholic Church kept secret our most sacred duty to love self and, as a result, made it impossible for people to love others. The darkness of that culture is being revealed daily by the sad revelations of sexual, physical and emotional abuse. We must learn and grow from these experiences and be determined that the solid foundation of love of self and others will not allow such neglect to occur again.

The wonder, uniqueness, goodness, individuality and genius of each child and adult needs to be affirmed in all of the social systems they inhabit. It is both an individual and collective responsibility to ensure regard, respect and equality for each person.

Social systems must ensure that no double standards exist and that some individuals, by virtue of their position, are not seen as more important than others. Status, wealth or education do not increase the worthiness of people, but there are many who believe they do, and the consequence is a snobbery that demeans others. Worthiness lies in your person, not in your behaviour. Behaviour, achievements and possessions are only experiences that come and go, but to make them the measure of your worth only darkens your own presence and that of others.

I believe that love of self and others is essential, practical and expedient if we are to live in harmony with each other.

## Q3. HOW CAN I BEST MAINTAIN MY RELATIONSHIP WITH SELF?

We cannot make any real progress within ourselves and outside ourselves in the realm of relationships, work, community, invention and creativity unless we regularly reflect. Reflection is the *sine qua non* of maturity and wisdom. However, its rarity does not mean we do not know of its vital importance. On the contrary, there is an even deeper knowing that realises the 'dangers' of reflection and seeks to distract us from such a process. Reflection invites us to be real, to see the wood from the trees, to be authentic, to be daring, and most of all to be true to ourselves. What a perilous world that is – to be real and true to one's own unique self in a world that largely invites us to be conformist. To *con-form* means to take on a false form, a shadow self that hides not only your unique self, but also the reality and truth of many unhappy situations in relationships, family, workplaces, community, church, classroom and school. How threatening it is to stand up and be yourself and real to parents who live their lives for you or through you or whose expectations are *un-realistic* or who dominate and control your life. How difficult it is to confront a teacher on behaviour that lessens your presence or to just ask to be respected at all times. How daunting it is to assert your sacred presence in a workplace where the ethos puts emphasis on productivity over people. And what about questioning religious beliefs or challenging medical or other consultants on their assessments? Not easy! To be real means risking being ostracised, ridiculed, marginalised, labelled as 'radical', 'difficult', 'selfish', being at the receiving end of aggression or losing what were important relationships. When people live in defensive worlds, the most frightening thing for them is to encounter a realist, somebody who speaks the truth of what he perceives, feels, believes and witnesses. It is not that those in defence want to directly hurt the person who tries to be authentic, but they do want to ensure that their defences and what lies hidden behind them are not shown up. People who conform and live their lives according to what they perceive as others' expectations are highly threatened by individuals who attempt to be real. One woman put it very well when she said to me: 'My family is unreal.' This 'unreal' tag can be applied to many social systems.

To reflect is to try to discover what is real. Interestingly, a common characteristic of a person who attempts to be true to self is resistance to conformity. Why is this mature way of being not modelled, encouraged and supported in families, schools, churches, communities and governments? The simple answer is fear, and unless individuals, and particularly those in positions of leadership – priests, teachers, politicians, community leaders and so on – free themselves of their fears, it is unlikely that reflection and being real will emerge as a way of living out our lives.

Recently I was working with some 600 adolescents on the whole issue of being true to oneself. At one point I asked them: 'In this school how much time per week do you get to reflect on such issues as: "Who am I?"; "What do I feel about self?"; "How do I feel my parents view me and how do I view them?"; "What does friendship mean to me?"; "How do I feel about being a member of this school?"; "Am I taking the subjects that really interest me?"; "Why do I regularly 'put down' that particular student?"; "What makes me sad and tearful at times?"' The answer was that they had no time for such reflection. But you cannot make wise choices, create real relationships, know and love self, discover the self of others and do what is true for you unless you reflect!

On one of the evenings over the days of working with the students, the parents and teachers came to hear me speak on the topic of 'The Self and Addictions'. I pointed out to the audience that whilst I realised that their main concerns were alcohol and drug addictions, I was more concerned about the most common addiction of all, which is the concern about what other people think of you! As with the students, I asked the parents and teachers: 'How much time daily do you give to reflection on such issues as:

- How do I feel about self?
- What is happening in my marriage?
- How come I have difficulty talking to my son?
- Why am I constantly irritable, cranky, tired, stressed, aggressive?
- How come I rarely stand up for myself?
- Do I feel fulfilled in my work?
- Why am I so overweight?
- Why don't I ever go to visit my parents?'

Many questions, many reasons to reflect – how much time? None! But how can progress be made within you, in your relationships, friendships, work, community and spirituality if you don't ask why, why, why? Of course the answer is staring us in the face – to reflect, to be real, will mean letting go of the many addictions that protect us from feeling empty, from anonymity – the addictions to success, to money, to prestige, to being liked, to alcohol, smoking, drugs, sex and endlessly giving to others. Sadly, these addictions are substitutes for the real thing, which is love of self and others and living your own unique life. Only the real thing can liberate you from your fears and addictions, and reflection is the invitation for each of us to take the road less travelled, the road of being true to self and others. It is not easy. We need all the support we can get and we need to actively seek that support.

## Q4. DOES HOW A PARENT FEELS ABOUT SELF AFFECT PARENTING?

'Know thyself' is an ancient dictum but it has timeless relevance to all of us, particularly to parents, teachers and other professional people who have the responsibility of the care and guidance of children. It is well established that how a parent feels about self influences everything he or she does, particularly how the children will feel about themselves.

However, it must not be forgotten that all significant adults in children's lives have an influence, especially grandparents, teachers, childminders, relatives and community leaders. All of these adults would do well to reflect both on how they feel about self and on how they relate to children.

There are two ways to reflect on these two issues: one is to look at how you typically treat self and how you interact with children. The second is to compare your daily actions to what you ideally need to do to feel good about self and to be an effective parent.

When you detect signs that you are putting yourself and/or your children down, it is important to see that these behaviours that demean self and children are opportunities, wake-up calls, to the realisation of self and the mature caring of children.

Self-esteem is revealed in all sorts of ways, but how you look after yourself in your everyday life is a major revelation of how you feel about yourself. Check the following list and see how you fare in this regard.

## CHECKLIST INDICATING SELF-NEGLECT

- Rushing and racing
- Missing meals
- Eating on the run
- Dependent on drugs (for example, Tagamet, tranquillisers, sleeping tablets, anti-depressants
- Working for long hours
- Frequently late for appointments
- Trying to do several things at once
- Rarely saying 'no' to demands made of you
- Having no time for self
- Few or no social outings

→

▫ Having little or no leisure time

▫ Lacking physical exercise

▫ Suffering from sleeplessness

▫ Overtired

▫ Rarely or never asking for help

▫ Overeating

▫ Undereating

▫ Dependent on alcohol

▫ Aggressive towards others

▫ Passive in the face of unrealistic demands or neglectful behaviours

▫ Manipulative

▫ Lacking caution (for example, don't wear seat-belt, drive with drink taken, carelessly cross busy thoroughfares)

▫ Having little family time

▫ Having to do everything perfectly

▫ Not taking care of your own or others' belongings

▫ Living in the future or in the past

▫ Fretful

▫ Worrying all the time

If you engage in one or more of the above behaviours, you are showing clear signs of poor regard for self. Clearly, the frequency, intensity and endurance of these behaviours are a further measure of the extent of self-neglect. An important further question to ask is how and to what extent are these daily ways affecting how you interact with your children. The following checklist may help you to identify how, from your place of self-neglect, you routinely interact with children. It is not that parents deliberately darken the presence of children, but they subconsciously act out from the darkness of their own interiority.

## CHECKLIST ON INEFFECTIVE PARENTING

- ☐ Shouting at children
- ☐ Ordering, dominating and controlling children
- ☐ Using sarcasm and cynicism as means of control
- ☐ Ridiculing, scolding, criticising
- ☐ Labelling children as 'bold', 'stubborn', 'stupid', 'lazy', 'no good'
- ☐ Threatening children that the parent will leave them
- ☐ Threatening to send children away
- ☐ Physically threatening children
- ☐ Being physically violent
- ☐ Assigning punishments out of proportion to misdemeanours
- ☐ Pushing, pulling and shoving children
- ☐ Comparing one child with another
- ☐ Having an obvious favourite in the family
- ☐ Not calling children by their first names
- ☐ Being too strict
- ☐ Expecting too much of children
- ☐ Showing no interest in children's welfare
- ☐ Letting children slide out of responsibility
- ☐ Not showing affection to children
- ☐ Punishing mistakes and failures
- ☐ Never apologising for mistakes
- ☐ Not saying 'please' and 'thank you' to children
- ☐ Being inconsistent and unpredictable in response to children's irresponsible behaviours
- ☐ Allowing the children to control the parent
- ☐ Withdrawing love from children
- ☐ Using hostile silences to attempt to control children

Whilst parents are not to be judged nor blamed for the above behaviours, they do have a responsibility *to* those actions that lessen children's presence. These signs point to parents' own neglect of themselves and their need to come into an acceptance of self, and from that solid base, to move towards positive rearing of their children.

Changing how you feel about yourself can only come about through an intense, enduring, loving, accepting and affirming relationship with yourself. Indeed, the very actions towards children that will raise their self-esteem are the same as those that parents need to show to themselves. 'Love your child as yourself' is in keeping with the Christian message of 'Love your neighbour as yourself'. What children need of parents and what parents need of themselves are:

- Unconditional love
- Acceptance
- Physical holding
- Nurturance
- Praise of effort
- Affirmation of uniqueness
- Listening
- Time
- Challenge
- Positive talk
- Kindness
- Support
- Humour
- Positive firmness
- Advice on request
- Compassion
- Belief in
- Emotional responsivity
- Emotional expression

- Encouragement
- Fairness
- Apology when wrong

Parents' relationship with self is an endless process that needs to be consistently worked on at all times. The presence of parent self-care guarantees care of children.

### Q5. I KNOW I'M VERY CONTROLLING IN A RELATIONSHIP. WHAT CAN I DO TO CHANGE THIS DEFENSIVE PATTERN OF RELATING?

There are many ways to control a partner, a child, an employee, a student, a friend and so on. The more typical ways are dominance, aggression, perfectionism, stubborn clinging to a point of view, intolerance, looking after the needs of others, being disappointed when expectations are not met, unrealistic demands, possessiveness and the tendency to become aggressive when opposed or confronted. Many people view such behaviours as 'normal', but the reality is that these actions are masking unresolved deep insecurities.

When one person is attempting to control another in a relationship, he or she either subconsciously does not see the manipulation or is not in a secure enough place to admit to it. Indeed, the reasons given are made to appear like love. For instance, a husband who controls his wife would argue: 'Is it not loving to protect your partner, look out for her interests, take charge of her wants and desires?' For many individuals this passes as genuine love.

A still not uncommon occurrence is a husband keeping all knowledge about finances away from his wife. She is not allowed to see bank statements or use the cheque book and she has no knowledge of his precise income. Any attempt on her part to earn her own money is dismissed. Certainly, women have come to a greater level of self-respect and will now quickly see that what her husband wants to do is control her. What she might not see is the enormous insecurity that lies hidden behind the controlling behaviour. Even when a woman spots that insecurity, she is in danger of counter-controlling if she attempts to take responsibility for her husband's insecurity. The way she could do that is by giving in to his ways and mothering him, thereby rendering him further helpless to any possibility of resolving his fears. Of course the wife has to look to her own hidden insecurity because why else would she need for him to become emotionally dependent on her.

The real test is when the person doing the controlling, by whatever means, is requested to give up those actions. Imagine the man who controls the finances being requested to equalise the situation and divulge all his financial affairs to his wife, so that she may share in spending the money, taking a portion of it as her own, free and clear, without having to account for it! Imagine, too, a parallel situation where a woman who controls her husband by always attending to his every need is requested to allow her partner to take more responsibility for his own needs and for her to begin to express more clearly her own needs! Such confrontations would certainly expose the lack of love that these controlling behaviours are hiding, but they would not resolve the fears and insecurities that underlie the respective targeted behaviours. The latter can only happen when the person controlling is ready to see the source of his or her behaviour. Considerable safety and love are needed for that to happen.

Control is the way your shadow self attempts to manage the problem of fear. Whenever any one of us engages in a controlling action, you can be sure that the hidden issue, usually subconscious, is any one of the following:

- You are fearful of being rejected
- You are fearful of conflict
- You are fearful of failing
- You are fearful of succeeding
- You are fearful of feeling helpless
- You are fearful of being wrong
- You are fearful of being annihilated

None of the fears makes you a 'bad' person or a 'weak' one. These fears manifest experiences you endured when you were a child and are now terrified of re-experiencing. There are very few of us who are not faced with such fears. However, it is only when we cannot admit to their existence that we resort to control. Sadly, the very experiences we hope to keep at bay are much more likely to recur in a controlling relationship. Your real self wants to be free and, somehow, will eventually create the opportunity for you to free yourself of your fears. The end of the need to control another begins when you see that control is incompatible with love and that the love and acceptance of self is the solid basis for togetherness.

## Q6. WHAT DOES IT MEAN FOR A PERSON TO ESTABLISH BOUNDARIES IN A RELATIONSHIP?

Boundaries are the firm behavioural lines you draw around respect for self and the other person. Any behaviour that is in any way unfair, controlling, aggressive or violent needs to be responded to with a very definite 'no' and an assertion of the right to respect. What needs to be very clear to the person who engages in aggressively controlling endeavours to get his own way is that such behaviour will not at any time gain him what he wants. It is good to know that a defensive behaviour only remains as long as it works. I have witnessed many men who had used violence as their weapon of control and when their partners or, indeed, children, colleagues or friends, broke the silence on their violence, these men quickly dropped their aggressive ways. Such a response is always welcome but the mere dropping of a defensive weapon does not resolve the deeper issues of insecurity and poor regard for self and others. These issues need to be tackled through the relationship with self and the relationships that have experienced the aggressive behaviours. However, the absence of the aggressively controlling behaviours that have been described makes it easier for mature relating to emerge.

Establishing boundaries needs to be done in a way that does not in any way lessen the presence of the person who aggressively infringes on the rights of others; if this were the case it would be a case of 'the pot calling the kettle black'. There is little chance of resolution when respect for the person who perpetrates the threatening actions is not present. It is not easy but it is necessary. It helps to see that the person who is outrageously demanding is masking major insecurities and fears.

When it comes to putting boundaries in place in the face of verbal aggression and the verbal threat of violence, be it adult, child or adolescent, the following actions are required:

- A clear statement: 'I'm not responding to being intimidated by your aggressive or manipulative behaviours.'
- When threatening behaviours persist, physically remove yourself from the situation.
- Maintain determination that you cannot afford to 'give in' to the threatening behaviours.

▢ When the situation has calmed, express an openness to listening, but only as long as the encounter is mutually respectful.

▢ When, in spite of following the above suggestions, the intimidating behaviours persist, seek professional help for yourself.

You might say that the last suggestion is unfair as 'surely it is the person who is doing all the threatening that needs professional help?' Indeed, but while you can offer the opportunity of professional help to the person concerned, it is vital that he makes the decision to go himself. Nevertheless, your seeking professional guidance is a recognition that there is a responsibility to take care of yourself and it makes it easier for the person who engages in aggressively controlling actions to seek help as well. There is also the issue that you may not have set definite boundaries around respect for self and others over the years and you now require help and support to do just that.

When it comes to establishing boundaries in the face of violent controlling, there is only one step to be taken and that is zero tolerance. No matter what the reasons are that lie behind such behaviour, the insecurities of one person cannot be allowed to create tyranny within a relationship. Whether the violent actions are towards others or self or a destruction of property, immediate help and refuge must be sought from somebody who can be strongly supportive and a recourse to instigating appropriate legal sanctions has to be made.

When it comes to children, adolescents or young adults, many parents balk at seeking the help of the police and the courts, even though their offspring may be engaging in violence towards their parents, taking drugs, drinking illegally, being destructive of property, refusing to go to school and so on.

These parents say, 'How could I do that to my son or daughter?' A similar situation can arise between a couple where one partner is being violated. Not only have these parents or partners abdicated their responsibility for care of self, but they have also ceased to be effective in the care of their children or partner, whichever is the case. Everyone loses out when firm and respectful boundaries are not put solidly in place.

## Q7. CAN YOU EXPLAIN THE CONCEPT OF 'EMOTIONAL INTELLIGENCE'?

The concept of emotional literacy or emotional intelligence is fast gaining currency. It is true to say when we hear the term 'emotional intelligence' we no longer wonder what it can refer to, even though we might find it difficult to define exactly what it is. Certainly, the need to develop emotional literacy has seeped into our consciousness and even into educational curricula, not only because emotional illiteracy poses major threats to our physical health, but also because it can play havoc with our internal and external worlds.

Emotional literacy means being able to identify, value, own and, when necessary, express all feelings. It also means being receptive to the expression of feelings from others. It means recognising the difference between welfare and emergency feelings and valuing both the former (love, joy, confidence, enthusiasm, tenderness, compassion) and the latter (fear, anger, depression, guilt, jealousy). It means recognising that emergency feelings within self or expressed by another are messages about unmet needs or buried conflicts. It involves knowing that feelings run deeply and that one feeling can mask another (for example, anger covering up hurt). Most of all, it means acknowledging our feelings and those of others so that we can recognise the ways in which our emotions influence how we think and act in this world.

Emotions that go unregistered, unrecognised and unquestioned, or emotions expressed without reflection on their meaning and purpose, are costly. Costly for the individual, who may use all sorts of substances or actions (such as food, drugs, alcohol, violence) to quell feeling ill at ease, but costly also for those who live with such an individual. Being at the receiving end of unprocessed feelings manifested in such behaviours as bullying, hypercriticism, disruptive behaviours and perfectionism can affect the receiver's self-esteem, group effectiveness, learning, work and self-confidence.

There is no doubt that your emotions are the most accurate barometer of how you are feeling about yourself, others and the world. To be out of touch with your own feelings or the feelings of others means continuously missing out on important opportunities to mature.

It has been thought that men are 'emotionally illiterate' and that women could be credited with emotional literacy. While it is true that men have been poorer when it comes to emotional literacy, it has to be asked how male children who receive 90 per cent of their parenting from women emerge into adulthood out of touch with their feelings? It is too easy to say they have followed in their fathers' footsteps, as the same phenomenon is true for male children reared by a female lone parent. The explanation may lie in the fact that while women are certainly comfortable in the expression of most feelings (except anger), they are decidedly uncomfortable in emotional responsivity. Women do shower their male children with a lot of affection, but they do not encourage them to express welfare and emergency feelings and, indeed, observation reveals that, quite subconsciously, women steer their male children away from nurturing and emotional tasks of showing comfort, support, warmth, care, sensitivity and compassion to others.

It would appear that both men and women have a major challenge in developing emotional literacy, but the task for men is to practise emotional expression and for women to become more emotionally receptive. Only when adults, parents, teachers and other significant adults in children's lives become fully emotionally literate, can children, both male and female, become emotionally adept.

## Q8. HOW CAN I BEST DEAL WITH MY ANGER?

Next to the welfare feeling of love, the emergency feeling of anger is the most important feeling that helps us to move forward in life. Anger is well termed as an 'emergency' feeling, as it alerts you to the presence of some threat to your well-being and your need to take corrective action. Many people have major difficulties in expressing anger, and as a result they tend to either under-express or over-express their anger. The former are fearful and the latter are forceful in that they attempt to control others (rather than self) through anger.

Those who suppress their anger employ passivity and people-pleasing to appease their own or another's anger. Because they do not use the energy of anger to express their needs, beliefs, worthiness and grievances, their growth remains static.

Equally, those who express their anger through verbal or physical aggression do not move forward and remain stuck in a vicious cycle of insecurity.

Many people, including professionals, confuse anger with aggression. Anger is a feeling and cannot hurt anyone; aggression is an action (verbal, physical, written) and can be seriously threatening to the security of others.

I remember a client who complained of abdominal pain.

'Do you express anger?' I asked.

'Yes, all the time. I'm aggressive at work and frequently fly off the handle at home.'

'What about your mother, do you show her anger?'

'Oh no, it would really upset her. And yet it is she that causes me to feel angry. So instead I take it out on everybody else.'

It definitely would be the case that her mother would not be in a mature place to understand a sudden onslaught of anger directed towards her, but the truth behind this daughter-mother situation is that it is the daughter who has to change, not the mother.

The woman described her mother as 'perfectionistic', 'fussy' and 'for whom you could do nothing right'. And yet the daughter continued to visit her mother with the sub-conscious hope that sometime she would receive approval and hence love from her mother.

'She makes me so angry,' she complained. But I pointed out to her that it is more appropriate to say that 'I feel angry at myself for allowing her to rule my life'.

Anger is the fire of the emotions; it is the power that will help us to move forward. Anger says: 'You must do some-thing about this untenable situation'. In this woman's case she saw that her dependence on approval from her mother needed to be outgrown and that she was now an adult who could approve of and love herself.

As the woman internalised and lived out this awareness, her attitude towards her mother gradually changed. She began to see that her mother had no sense of her own worthiness and therefore found it difficult to approve of others.

As the daughter's feelings of self-worth grew, her stomach pains disappeared and she was able to give praise and affection to her own children and spouse and to her mother. The latter dynamic eased the hostility between them.

It is important that the emergency feeling of anger is turned into something creative that can be used for personal growth.

An example of threatening expressions of anger from another are seen when a husband shouts at his wife who is sick in bed. Nine times out of ten, the source of the husband's anger is fear. He is dependent on his wife and relies on her to be strong and cannot bear the idea that he may have to cope alone. It is not uncommon for such husbands to die before their wives, even if their wives were seriously ill before them.

It is still a sad situation that the socialisation of male children leads to them having to hide their true feelings rather than expressing their fears and anxieties.

Expression of all feelings, including anger, needs to start with the words 'I feel . . . ', and not 'You make me . . . ' When you own your feelings you are likely to see the opportunities for growth that they present.

Nobody can make you do anything. In the end, whether consciously or subconsciously, the decision is yours.

## Q9. HOW DO I PREPARE FOR PARENTING AND WHAT SHOULD I LOOK OUT FOR WHEN CHOOSING A CHILDMINDER?

It is now well documented that poor parenting skills and parents having a poor to moderate sense of themselves can affect the emotional, social, intellectual and physical development of children. This is not a deliberate failure in parenting but one that arises from the unresolved vulnerabilities of parents. Sadly, it is still the case that parenting is not regarded as a profession and does not benefit from the three training 'I's' of other professions: initiation, induction and in-service training. Initiation is best done before starting a family and involves education in parenting skills and parents' own self-development. Initiation is crucial, as knowledge of parenting skills is not sufficient to ensure effective parenting. Parents can only execute such skills when they have become effective in the caring of their individual selves and each other (where there are two parents).

The induction phase involves having the emotional and advisory support of a mentor for at least the first one to two years of parenting. The old tradition of young parents relying on their parents of origin was not necessarily wise, as many problems in their homes were perpetuated in the new family unit. What makes for good parenting and mentoring is not blood but emotional maturity.

The third phase of professional training is in-service education. This consists of training in-situ, particularly when problems in parenting occur. Family dynamics never stay constant as the family moves from stages of having very young, to young, adolescent and early adult offspring. Parents themselves change also and where there are two parents, their couple relationship will have changed as well. Bringing an expert into the family situation could do wonders for its wellbeing, far faster than talking at one remove.

Not only do parents influence the development of children, but teachers, relatives and siblings can also have profound effects. An uncharted area is the effect of childminders on children. The Louise Woodward case has highlighted this issue. Nowadays, children can spend more time with childminders than with parents, especially in the crucial formative years from infancy to five years of age. Considerable thought needs to go into the selection of a childminder, and too often convenience for the working parents is a criterion that determines choice. However, you must consider the parenting skills of the minder. Certainly, recognised training in child-minding would be a reassuring asset but bear in mind that education does not equal maturity and the ability to care.

Observe the childminder's interaction with your children over a period of at least a week before you return to work. This is far more reliable than interviews, diplomas, references, hearsay and curriculum vitae. Look for qualities that will ensure that children feel safe, loved, challenged, encouraged and positively corrected when they transgress boundaries. Ability to listen and to communicate directly and clearly, both verbally and non-verbally, are important consid-erations, as is the maturity to be able to reveal problems when they occur and ask for help and support. Being at ease with physical contact is essential, as there is nothing stronger than the hug, the silent holding and the pat on the back to convince children they are loved.

Following your week having the childminder work alongside you, it helps to maintain your observation when you bring and collect the children from the childminder. Do also ask the childminder for feedback on how things went for the day and watch for any discrepancies between what is said verbally and what her body is saying. Tone of voice, speed of speech, facial expression, body posture and level of eye contact are far more accurate barometers of how things really were. Be sure to communicate that this is a partnership-in-parenting arrangement and that you are there to help, advise and support in any way possible. It is frequently the case that a parent will not question the practise of a childminder or communicate concerns for fear of upsetting the childminder. However, your priority is your child's security, and once you communicate in a way that is respectful, open, direct and supportive, then possibilities of causing offence are eliminated. When a minder reacts defensively to such positive inquiries, they are showing their inner vulnerabilities and this may be a source of concern for you. A random repeat of sharing and observing the caring would be a further means of guaranteeing a good choice of childminder. Finally, fair pay for fair care is a necessary consideration.

# CHAPTER TWO

# WHAT ROLES DO PARENTS NEED TO PLAY?

## INTRODUCTION

A recent Irish research report commissioned by the Ceifin Centre, Burren, Co. Clare, examined the factors that create family wellbeing. The study interviewed up to 250 children in different family types, all of whom were aged between eleven and sixteen. The study highlighted three major areas that determine family wellbeing:

- the quality of relationships within the family
- the level of self-esteem of each parent
- the degree to which conflict is resolved when it arises.

What is fascinating about the report is that the type of family was not a determining factor of family wellbeing. In many ways this is not surprising, because what happens between people in a family is much more important than the constitution of the family, whether that be a two-parent, one-parent, re-constituted or three-generation family. This is not to say that poverty and social deprivation are not hardships for any family. All parenting has to be about enhancing relationships, whether between parent and parent, parent and child, child and child, or outsider and child. By 'outsider' I mean those adults or, indeed, other children who cross the threshold of the family home. I have encountered several situations where, for example, grand-parents had an over-dominating influence on the family dynamics of a young family and the parents were not in a place of personal security to create strong boundaries to with-stand those distressing influences. A parent needs to establish that she is in charge of the family and be able to champion herself and her children when anybody poses a threat to family, wellbeing. Similarly, within the family, a mother or father needs to ensure that not only the parent-child relationships are of a positive nature but also child-child relationships. It is not uncommon for an older child to make a younger child's life difficult while the parent does nothing to correct such conflict.

Parents need to know how to create relationships that promote family wellbeing and, obviously, to spot ways of relating that block family wellbeing. Questions 1 to 3 and Question 12 explore some of these issues.

The role of fathers in families is a concern to many mothers and, indeed, to the children. There appears to be a growing awareness that men can be equally effective at parenting, but much more still needs to be done.

It is now common in most families, whether it is a two-parent or a single-parent family, for each parent to work outside the home. Integrating work and home life is challenging, and many parents experience guilt about the little time spent with children. Guilt often leads to over-compensating so that parents 'spoil' children with material things. This can lead to children having unrealistic expectations of parents and of other adults as well. It can often mean that those children who experience little love but lots of treats go on to continue to fill the void of not being seen and loved for self with material things. This becomes a bottomless pit, because there is no substitute for the real thing – in this case unconditional love. It is not the quantity but the quality of time spent with children that counts. I know of children who feel that their parent's career matters more than they do and this experience can lead to them hating work and losing motivation for career development. This can be puzzling for parents who are work-addicted and can lead to considerable family conflict.

Some parents experience confusion as to whether or not boys need to be reared differently to girls, and Question 10 below attempts to respond to that issue.

Parents need to know also about the influences of other people and social systems on their child's development. Individual teachers and the school ethos can positively or negatively impact on a child's life and it is important that parents keep a keen eye out for any signs of distress in their child. When a child's wellbeing is under threat outside the home, it is necessary that parents take appropriate action to restore a cycle of wellbeing to their child's life outside the home. Easier said than done, as many parents, because of their own lack of confidence, find it very difficult to confront the behaviour of a teacher or school that is blocking their child's emotional and educational progress. These parents need to confront the blocks inside themselves before they can effectively counter blocks outside themselves.

Other adults (grandparents, uncles, aunts, neighbours) can influence children's wellbeing, and noticing both their positive and negative responses to your child is an important exercise.

Marital separation and divorce are now commonplace and Question 7 explains how to minimise the effects of marital breakdown on children.

## Q1. ISN'T THE NOTION OF DEMOCRATIC PARENTING A WHOLE LOT OF NONSENSE?

A parent's basic concept of parenting is central to how effective she will be in guiding her children's development. Many parents still view parenting as a matter of controlling their children into what they see as right for them. However, there is considerable evidence that children are resisting this type of parenting at an alarming rate. Children who rebel at being controlled are brought to child guidance centres and counsellor's rooms by despairing parents in increasing numbers. Children dare to do today what their parents would never have thought of or dared to do to their parents.

What has changed? The challenge has emerged from the general cultural changes that have and continue to take place. Intuitively children sense the democratic atmosphere of our times and are much more likely to hold on to their dignity in the face of parents' and other adults' attempts at authority over them. When they exhibit their right to say 'no' to a request and the parent retaliates with 'you'll do as I tell you', a vicious cycle can develop in which the parents attempt to assert themselves and the children dig their heels in. They absolutely refuse to be dominated or coerced. Most attempts to subdue them are futile. Children are far more resilient in a conflict situation. They are not inhibited by social consequences of 'appearances' and are free of the time constraints that parents typically work under. Sadly, the home can become a battlefield where there is little cooperation and no harmony. Instead there is hostility, frustration and a feeling of helplessness on the part of the besieged parent.

Any time parents order a child to do something, or try to make him do it, they invite conflict. This does not mean that parents cannot guide or influence their children into responsible behaviour. What it does mean is that parents need to find a different and more effective approach. Parents, teachers and other adults need to let go of their authoritarian ways and assume a parenting approach that is respectful and effective. It is important that adults realise that while the old dominating methods may have been effective in bringing about compliance, they were not effective in raising children's self-esteem nor in teaching them self-control and self-responsibility. Indeed, the old methods induced fear, low self-esteem and helplessness in many children.

Many parents will claim that when they are being authoritarian it is for 'the child's good!' There are a number of ways to check whether or not this is the case:

- Is prestige involved?
- Do you want others to see what an obedient child you have?
- Do you have a sense of satisfaction when the child complies?
- Do you want to be known as 'good' parents?
- Do you want to feel that you have the 'upper' hand?
- Do you feel that the child 'should' obey you?

Another way to analyse your 'good' intentions is to look at what follows your interaction with the child. Does the child continue with the same difficult behaviour in spite of your attempts to gain compliance? Does he exhibit defiance? Do you feel angry, resentful and even more determined to gain control? Real giveaways are your body posture and the tone of your voice. Is your body tense and stiff? Are your arms folded across your chest? Is there fire in your eyes? Is your tone of voice commanding, aggressive, insistent, demanding? When your intentions are good your body will be relaxed and your tone of voice quietly firm.

Getting children to respond in a responsible way demands that parents re-evaluate their attitudes and the means used to bring about such a desirable situation. Certainly parents would do well to understand that the word 'authority' means 'authorship of self' and not control over another. Secondly, parents (and teachers) need to accept that they simply do not have authority over their children. Children know this, even though adults struggle to accept it. Parents can no longer demand, control and impose. Parents need to learn how to lead and how to stimulate. Most important is to be firm about what action *you* will take and not what you are going to make the child do. This is the cornerstone of effective parenting and leadership. The parent, as leader, assesses the demands of the situation and works towards fulfilling those demands, not his or her own preference. Understanding, listening, encouragement, logical consequences, mutual respect, respect for order, routine and gaining cooperation, all come into play in the quest for order.

Above all, the most important step is for the parent to be vigilant as to how he or she is acting in the situation. This is a difficult task: it is so easy to slip back into being authoritarian. Parents need to constantly remind themselves: 'I cannot force my children to do anything or stop them. I may try all the tricks in the book but I cannot force my child into cooperative action.' Responsible behaviour needs to be stimulated, not commanded. Parents can employ their ingenuity, creativity, tact, patience and sense of humour to promote cooperation.

Parenting in a democratic way is far more challenging than parenting by the mere use of force. The gains of the former far outweigh those of the latter approach: parents feel far more in control of themselves; their relationships with their children are far more harmonious and their children learn one of the principle goals of parenting – self-control.

## Q2. HOW COME MOST PARENTING IS DONE BY WOMEN?

There seems to be an assumption that men do not make effective childminders. The reverse side of this assumption is that women are effective at childminding. It is possible that what lies at the bottom of these assumptions is that women still do 90 per cent of the parenting of children and that in cases of separation women are still left holding the children.

There is also the fact that it is women who predominantly populate the caring professions – for example, social work, counselling, teaching, nursing, childcare, nursery teachers.

However, there seems to be an even more fundamental objection to men or male adolescents being employed as childminders – there is a strong mistrust of men around children. There is a prevailing negative attitude among parents, both male and female, to having a man looking after their children. At an even more extreme level there is the belief that men who want to look after children are perverted in some way or other. Indeed, there is the almost automatic assumption that male carers equal child abuse. This fear seems to run deep and, regrettably, this reinforces even more strongly that women are more effective at caring than men, even though there is no solid evidence for such a belief. The fact that women have long taken on the responsibilities of childcare does not mean that they are automatically better at it!

Another sad development is that many men are now reluctant to offer childcare services because they are open to accusations of child abuse far more than women.

Indications of the fear surrounding employing male carers are that even less than 1 per cent of au pairs are male, even though there are many males who seek such work. I know of no creches or nursery schools run by men.

Are there other issues that lead parents to cleave to the tradition that nobody wants a man to take care of their children or cook the meals or do the ironing? Certainly, the stereotyping of women as 'carers' and men as 'takers' has done much to keep men out of the playroom and the kitchen. The revelation, too, over the last decade, of the sexual violation of children by males has copper-fastened the notion that men are a danger to children. However, it is unfair to paint all men with that brush – there are many men who are excellent at taking care of children and there is no reason why other men could not learn the skills of effective child-management.

Caring for children is not a gender issue. Being female is no guarantee of effective childcare. Indeed, research shows that mothers hit children far more than men do! What determines quality childcare is the nature of the relationship that the parent or childminder has with the child, the parent's or childminder's own level of self-esteem and how good he or she is at conflict resolution.

There is an assumption that the feminine qualities of being able to provide warmth and affection, tenderness and kindness, physical and emotional nurturance and patience are sufficient for rearing children. However, the reality is that to be effective, women also need the masculine qualities of firmness, determination, the capacity to create definite boundaries and to provide children with opportunities for rough and tumble games and practical house maintenance (as opposed to domestic) skills.

It will be a tragedy if things remain as they are. Both women and men have the potential to develop the necessary feminine and masculine qualities needed for effective childrearing. Preparation for such a role is best done in the earliest years of all children's lives. Parents need to ensure that both female and male children are provided with the opportunities to develop both their feminine and masculine sides. There is considerable evidence that mothers unconsciously steer their male children away from the feminine-type responsibilities within the home and direct them towards masculine-type behaviours. The opposite happens for female children.

Men, too, need to assert their potential to be effective child-carers and not to be side-lined by women or, indeed, other men, or by threats of being accused of being 'soft', 'perverted', or a 'child abuser'. The individuals who pass such judgements need to similarly reflect on the dark source of such attitudes. That is not to say that, where children are concerned, due caution is not required; but caution and exclusion of men from their right to care for children are entirely different issues.

## Q3.  AREN'T WOMEN NATURALLY BETTER AT PARENTING THAN MEN?

Recently I read that research is proving that the reluctance men have with feelings and with communicating may have a biological root. The theory is that the emotional centres of a man's brain are located far more discreetly than in a woman's, and the two halves of the male brain are connected by a smaller group of fibres than in the female brain. The notion is that information flows less easily from the right (emotional) side to the left (verbal) side, so men tend to have difficulties expressing how they feel. I wonder how these writers would explain how rapidly men can touch into their anger!

What is highly questionable about the quoted research is that biological differences do not equal emotional and behavioural differences between the sexes. A second consideration is which comes first – the behavioural and emotional differences or the physical differences between the sexes? Furthermore, observation shows no differences in the emotional responses between male and female infants; it is only later on that differences begin to emerge. The fourth objection I have to the biological hypothesis is that not all men have difficulties in identifying and expressing their feelings and there are women who can be just as emo-tionally illiterate as men.

My own belief is that some men's difficulties with emotional expression lies in how they were brought up, what is expected of them and what is provided for them.

Parents can feel hurt, puzzled and guilty when the cute boys they doted on when they were little turn into the 'thugs' on the streets. Adults, both male and female, watch helplessly as the little boys they cuddled physically bully each other in the playground and sportsfield. Some parents have the sad experience of their male offspring becoming violent towards them and the other children in the family.

While many parents and teachers will battle against the idea that they interact with children on gender lines, nevertheless we are all gendered beings, and, whether consciously or unconsciously, we will treat infant girls and infant boys in a way that reflects our own understandings and experiences. A fascinating observation is that when we hear of a birth, the first question that comes to our lips is 'Is it a boy or a girl?' The answer to that question will immediately set us off on the quest of a 'gender appropriate' card and gift and we may be watchful of the individual parent's reaction to the gender of the baby.

It is not too difficult to observe how parents and other adults encourage certain characteristics in boys and others in girls. The differences in the ways adults physically relate to boys compared to girls is very obvious. For example, boys are breastfed for longer than girls and each feeding time is longer; they are weaned more slowly, potty trained later and held for longer periods of time. Even the language used to describe the difficult behaviours of boys and girls reflects differences in parenting. For example, a boy may be described as 'tough', a girl as a 'tomboy'; a boy as 'a cry-baby', a girl as 'over-sensitive'. Furthermore, parents use different words and tones of voice to soothe baby girls and baby boys.

It is at the level of emotional relating that the most profound effects of gender can be witnessed but ignored by adults. Within families, boys are not encouraged to take on responsibilities that involve tenderness and nurturance, nor are they encouraged to talk about their feelings. There is the added factor that whereas girls have a model in their mothers for emotional expression, boys do not have this advantage in having an equivalent emotionally literate male model. Indeed, boys risk serious ridicule when they go against what is seen as being typically 'male'. Girls have endless opportunities to practise the emotional skills of care, kindness, tenderness, nurturance and expression of upsetting feelings. On the other hand, boys' time and energies go into mastering physical skills and bottling up their feelings.

It is not that boys do not have feelings of love, fear, depression, sadness, jealousy and guilt, but they are rarely encouraged to identify, understand and express them. Neither are they encouraged to enter the emotional world of others.

The failure of homes, schools, communities and government social policies to equip boys with emotional literacy is having a serious effect on their emotional, physical and social welfare, and that of others. The increasing violence on our city streets is a stark pointer to our failure. Men commit 90 per cent of violent crimes and 90 per cent of prison inmates are male. Surely the little boys we love so much deserve the opportunities to explore the expansiveness of emotionality and not to be condemned later on to finding emotional expression through aggression and violence.

## Q4. ARE TWO-PARENT FAMILIES BETTER FOR CHILDREN THAN SINGLE-PARENT FAMILIES?

Divorce and separation are generally bad news for children. So, too, statistically, is being a member of a family other than one led by two parents of different sexes. Simply put, there is nothing to compare to a two-parent stable family. However, this kind of family is becoming less and less a reality.

In Europe, between one-in-four and one-in-three marriages end in seperation/divorce. What is even more alarming is that the interval between marriage and separation/divorce is narrowing, indicating that children are not enjoying a long period of settled family life. For example, in Britain 25 per cent of all women in their thirties are divorced. The loss of a parental figure, usually the father, along with the break-up of the family home and battles about money and access to children are occurring earlier.

Single parenthood is rising inexorably. Between 30 and 40 per cent of all pregnancies occur outside marriage, the highest rate being in the main cities. Furthermore, teenage pregnancy is on the rise. Teenage pregnancy, inadequate parenting, poverty and crime chase each other in a vicious cycle of cause and effect.

In Britain a third of all marriages end in divorce and one in four families with children is headed by a single parent.

More and more research is showing that many children from fragmented or newly cobbled together families are troubled, troublesome and seriously depressed. Some are deeply disturbed. Not surprisingly, these children do not do well at school. When you are troubled in your heart, it is very difficult to be involved in the affairs of the head.

A recent OECD study found that the children of broken families are 40 per cent more likely to achieve poorly in school. Another report that looked at the effects of divorce and separation on children drew the bleak conclusion that children of separated families tend to gain fewer academic qualifications as well as being more likely to leave school and home early. They are also more likely to engage in anti-social or criminal behaviour and are more likely to resort to smoking, drinking and illegal drug use.

However, research is routinely ignored, and it is difficult to persuade parents, teachers, politicians, the media and the public that divorce and its results do affect children's physical, emotional and social welfare and their education. It is difficult for those weighed down with the guilt of divorce 'baggage' to face the truth, even when it is staring them in the face.

What is to be done? There is no suggestion here that unhappy couples should stay together for the children's sake. Such a sacrifice can often put an intolerable burden on the shoulders of the children, not to mind the parents themselves. Certainly, with an eye to preventing turmoil in children's lives, more serious consideration needs to be given to choosing to have children. This holds true both for couples and for single parents. The level of maturity of the adult is a crucial consideration, as well as the stability of the couple relationship for those couples who choose to have children. Education for parenting is also essential.

But what actions are needed for those children who are the victims of the conflictual family situation? In the case of single parents who have chosen to be without a partner, they need to seek all the support and help they can get. Many communities now have a Family Resource Centre which is supportive of all families in distress. For the two-parent family, where parents have chosen to split up, there is a need for the recognition of the fact that marital breakdown does not have to mean family breakdown. What is needed is an amicable parting, the maintenance by each parent of strong bonds of contact with each of the children, and a visible cooperation between the parents in the management of the family. Concern and involvement in the children's education are also needed.

What is frequently missed in the situation where a two-parent family becomes a one-parent family and the other parent, usually the father, has limited access rights, is the provision of opportunities for the children to voice their distress and any needs that arise from their upset lives. It is also wise to involve the school in supporting the children of separated families. Indeed, schools may be the place where children, through personal development classes, can be given opportunities to 'act out' their distress. There is certainly an urgent need for society to acknowledge and address the fall-out of marital breakdown on the lives of children.

## Q5. ARE FATHERS CAPABLE OF PARENTING?

Fathers are often perceived by their children as remote, absent or neglectful. It was not too long ago that a father's limited role was to bring in the money, carve the Sunday joint and be the final arbiter or authority a mother called upon to discipline the children.

Direct emotional expression between fathers and children as a way for the children to get to know their father and themselves was not encouraged. Indeed, the opposite was the case and still is to a large degree. It is not just boys who lose out in the lack of a heart-to-heart relationship with their fathers; girls also have an equal longing for a father to show love and to put them first before work, sports and the pub. When children feel they have not managed to capture their father's attention and love, they protectively conclude they are not good enough. As a consequence, girls, when adult, will lack confidence in their ability to attract men, and boys will feel emotionally unsure of themselves when with their own gender and have an emotional illiteracy when pursuing intimacy with the opposite sex.

Another way in which boys manifest their anguish over the continually 'absent' father is by their identification of their sense of worth with work. Work is often one of the few ways they have to get their father's approval, and it comes as no surprise that among men there is a high level of addiction to work. On the other hand, girls learn to impress their fathers by repeating their mother's behaviour of 'taking care' of their fathers, but not asking anything from their fathers.

Ironically, there is considerable evidence to show that when parents separate, fathers begin to have a more enriching experience of what it means to be a father. Instead of relying on the relationship via the children's mother, taking that relationship for granted or not rocking the boat of that coalition, fitting in and being occasionally helpful, they now have time to create the relationship with their children directly. They have opportunities too to get to know their children and for their children to get to know them in ways that challenge them, rather than adapting to the limited framework in which they related before.

It is not my intention to suggest that marriages need to break down before men enter more fully into fathering their children. On the contrary, there is nothing compared to the two-parent stable family, where each parent directly creates a relationship with each child. It is not that fathers do not have the capacity to be emotionally expressive nor, indeed, that mothers do not have the capacity to be emotionally receptive, but both fathers and mothers need to create opportunities for the two-way street that loving children is all about. It is important that mothers support and encourage fathers to be emotionally expressive and that fathers support mothers to be emotionally receptive. It is a truism that men have difficulty with direct emotional expression; it is also a truism that many women have difficulties in emotional receptivity. In other words, men may be poor in expressing love and women may be poor at receiving love. Both inhibitions affect children's perceptions of themselves.

It would be easy to say that women have kept men out of the emotional relating that is the cornerstone of effective parenting, but men need to strongly assert their right to greater emotional intimacy with their children. Equally, women need to assert their need to share the task of parenting and to learn to express their own needs to receive warmth, nurturance and affection. Again, not surprisingly, the addiction to caring is still common among women. However, there are signs of change. For example, in Australia in the next five years, 45 per cent of women will choose not to marry and have children. Furthermore, in Great Britain, one in two marriages are breaking down and 70 per cent of these split-ups are initiated by the female partner.

It is also the case in Great Britain that by age thirty, 40 per cent of women are divorced or separated and few have any inclination to re-marry. In Ireland similar social trends are evolving. I believe these startling social changes are a cry out to men for equality in family and domestic responsibilities. If the challenge is taken up by both men and women to create equality in both marital and family settings, then everybody will gain – men, women, children and society. However, if we ignore the symptoms of inequality, then the family as the bedrock of a progressive society is seriously at risk.

## Q6. DOES ROUGH-AND-TUMBLE PLAY WITH FATHERS HELP CHILDREN IN ANY WAY, BECAUSE I HATE IT?

New research findings suggest that rough horseplay with fathers helps boys to learn self-control. It would appear that the discouragement of such behaviour by some psychologists in the 1960s may have been misguided. My own view is that fathers play-fighting with their children indicates an involvement by fathers in their families and, rather than being frowned upon, it deserves encouragement. It is good for children, both male and female, to experience the power of their bodies and a sense that they can stand up for themselves. However, rough play with children must not cross the line into aggression, and on this issue the new studies indicate that fathers who combined boisterous play with a firm but *not harsh* approach to discipline had the most effective relationships with their children. The researchers seemed surprised that the sons of these fathers were often the most popular boys in their class. Furthermore, even boys aged three to four who were close to their dads and played roughly with them were rated as the most popular in class. The danger in interpreting the results of these studies is that rather than the play-fighting being the determinant of these children's popularity, it could be the fathers' involvement and interest per se in their children. Certainly, the fact that 'harshness' was not an aspect of the play-fighting indicates that the children perceived their father's involvement with them as a manifestation of his love and interest in them. Indeed, it is the intention of a behaviour that counts most and children intuitively pick up when the intent is loving or hostile. Once fathers who play-fight respect their children's physical boundaries and don't force their physical playing on them, I have no difficulty with such interactions.

I am wary of another conclusion of the studies that suggests boys learn self-control from the rough-and-tumble play with their fathers. A number of questions arise from such a conclusion, not least the one regarding the high percentage of boys who are reared in single-female-parent families. If it is true that boys learn self-control through rough-and-tumble play with their fathers, how is this to be achieved in the single-female-parent situation? It is too simplistic an explanation. It is more accurate to view self-control as a product of high self-esteem, and children who are emotionally secure do experience being well-liked by their peers and teachers. Security arises from the experience of being consistently loved by a parent, no matter what the type of family. When love is not present or a child is faced with non-involvement or a critical, impatient and irritable kind of parenting, then all sorts of defences are created by the child to reduce these threats to wellbeing.

The other question that arises from these new research findings, which talk only about play-fighting between fathers and their sons, is what about girls and their fathers? Girls also enjoy friendly rough-and-tumble play and can be just as hardy as boys. There is a danger that the interpretation of the research findings may contribute further to the polarisation of male and female children and perpetuate the stereotypical notion that 'boys will be boys' and 'girls will be girls'. Such notions go against other findings that show that female soldiers can be fiercer than their male counterparts.

The studies also pose the danger of polarising fathers and mothers. Men and women equally are capable of play-fighting, and if a friendly rough-and-tumble is good for a child's wellbeing then it is incumbent on both mothers and fathers to engage in such interactions. However, I sincerely doubt that physical familiarity which is not couched in warmth and affection will do much for a child's security. Talking with, playing, hugging, embracing and showing interest in the child's world are equally vital parts of a father's and a mother's involvement with children.

Incidentally, for those parents who worry that toy weapons predispose children to violence, it is my experience that it is not the toy guns but feelings of rejection in children that lie at the root of violence. At the heart of violence lies deep hurt and the unfulfilled longing to be loved.

## Q7. MY HUSBAND AND I HAVE SEPARATED AND I AM WORRIED ABOUT THE EFFECTS OF THE DIVORCE ON THE CHILDREN. HOW CAN I MINIMISE THESE EFFECTS?

Research now clearly shows that it is not divorce that is irrevocably blocking of children's emotional security but the nature of the relationships that exist between ex-partners and between parents and children before the break-up. There is little doubt that each parent suffers considerably when continuous unresolved conflict eats not only into the heart of the relationship, but also into the heart of their own self-belief, regard and confidence. Children, too, inevitably are adversely affected when their parents' relationship is disharmonious (to say the least) and each parent, because of their own inner and marital turmoil, may find it difficult to notice or respond to the manifestations of their children's distress. Children often wish for and support their parents' separation but are often ill-prepared for the profound disruption that occurs when their parents finally separate. Even when the children remain in the family home – nine times out of ten with their mother – family routine, family ethos and responsibilities change radically. It is an established fact that separated mothers have major difficulties in the management of the challenging behaviour of their adolescent sons, and the absence of the father as the arbiter or authority a mother calls upon in order to discipline a child can be sorely missed. There can be financial constraints and there is the difficulty for children in explaining to friends. Many children question their own contribution to the break-up, and, particularly when conflict between parents continues after the relationship ends, they tend to blame themselves. After all, when parents continue to fight after they part, children often ask me 'what then was the real reason why they separated?' Children also have to negotiate a whole new relationship with their father, who, up to the break-up, may have relied on his partner to carry the emotional responsibilities within the family. It is certainly a truism that in an unhappy relationship a mother rarely abandons her children on a daily basis in the same way that a father can. This is true before and after the separation. However, what is encouraging is that divorce is presenting fathers with the opportunities to get to know their children in ways that were not available when the family dynamic was largely mediated by the mother. However, it has to be said that whilst 30 per cent of fathers disappear, mothers rarely if ever do.

While divorce presents opportunities for everybody in the family to grow individually and collectively, the first two years of the break-up are painful for all. However, though bleak in the short-term, the long-term prospects can be considerably better than what existed pre-divorce.

Each parent has a major responsibility to recover a sense of self following the break-up. This is not easy, as feelings of grief, loneliness, rage, panic, despair and resentment can be overwhelming. It takes patience and time to (re)discover a sense of self and to create new supports.

In order for the family to benefit from the break-up of the marriage, the separated parents needs to be determined to resolve or at least accept their differences and to engage with each other in respectful and friendly ways. Certainly, this display of mature contact needs to exist when they are with the child or children, or making arrangements about them or discussing financial, educational and other family issues. It does children no end of good when they witness their separated parents being friendly with each other. Children see that it is not a disaster when relationships fail and that there is life for everyone after their parents part. It would be considerably supportive of each parent if they would extend their being bonded by friendship rather than resentment to all their interactions, not just when children are present.

Parents need to be prepared for a time that children may not want to see the parent who leaves the family home, and they should not slip into coercing the child to visit that parent. What is important is that the parent who has left does all in his power to consistently maintain the relationship so that the child eventually realises that 'I'm important to my dad, and that my dad misses me'. Getting cross about the difficult situation will only convince the child that he is a burden and not a joy in the parent's life.

Divorce, then, rather than being a time of continued conflict, can be transformed into a time of opportunities for change for all members of the family.

## Q8. ISN'T IT BETTER FOR CHILDREN THAT MOTHERS STAY AT HOME, AT LEAST FOR THE FIRST THREE TO FOUR YEARS?

There is a new trend in America for well-educated mothers to choose to stay at home with the children, at least during the pre-school years. It is only a matter of time before this development reaches our shores. There is no suggestion here that it is something new for career women to choose to stay home with the kids, but the twist in the tale is that this new band of American homemakers are being evangelical about domesticity and claiming that being a homemaker is much more fulfilling than forging a career.

These women are suggesting that modern women have lost touch with motherhood, and they encourage women to become part of the family again. I do not think that women who manage career and family commitments will be too pleased with the criticism that they have lost the motivation to parent their children. After all, it is not the quantity of time you spend with children that matters but the quality. There are many stay-at-home mothers I have encountered over the years who did not parent effectively and there are those mothers I know who have effectively managed home and career very well. The true barometer of effective parenting is a mother's (or father's) relationship with self; as I have already mentioned, clinical and research studies show that a parent can only bring a child to the same level of personal realisation they have reached themselves. Inevitably a parent brings his or her emotional baggage into the family and the extent of a parent's insecurity is a strong determinant of how well he or she parents children.

While I agree that it is a mother's right to choose to stay at home or develop a career, I am puzzled as to why those American women who are choosing to stay at home have to convince others that the right thing to do is to stay home with the children? When a mother has attained a reasonable degree of maturity, I certainly believe it benefits both child and mother when the mother stays at home during the pre-school years, but not to the extent that it becomes a law for women to stay at home. Convincing others that stay-at-home mothers are on a higher moral ground smacks to me of 'me thinks she protests too much'. Why not quietly make your own decision; what need lies behind the broadcasting of this decision? Is it that these women are not quite convinced of their decision and need the support of others? This is not surprising given that not too long ago women who stayed at home were not accorded much social status. Indeed, parenting is still not seen as a profession, and recent research in Britain concluded that mothers who give up their careers lose social status, while career women continue to build up social status. There is no more self-sacrificing profession than that of parenting, and I have equal regard for the parent who chooses to stay at home and the parent who chooses to maintain a career, once they fulfil their responsibilities towards their children. It seems to me that the decision to stay at home or to maintain a career is a deeply personal and individual one and any crusade makes it difficult for a woman to come to her own decision. Whether the feminist movement is being evangelical about mothers having careers or enjoying home life, there is an attempt to sway the individual woman a particular way, rather than encouraging her to make her own decision. Right now there is an emerging conflict between those women who want to stay at home and those who want to go out working. This polarisation is not helpful to the emancipation of women.

A disturbing aspect of this new crusade is that there is no mention of fathers. Surely if men and women are to be equal, then a father also has the right to choose to stay at home with children! Is it not only fair that in a two-parent family there should be a negotiation on who stays at home with the children, rather than automatically assuming that it be the mother? I was amused to read that one of the leading women crusaders said that 'Men do seem to be rather hopeless at laundry.' Some men may not have been given the opportunities during their upbringing to develop domestic skills, but that does not mean they are not capable of learning such skills. The suggestion, too, that women are more empathic is insulting, as men, too, when given the opportunities, are quite capable of manifesting their feminine side. In any case, effective parenting is about possessing a balance of both masculine and feminine qualities. Women who are high on femininity and low on masculinity and men who are high on masculinity and low on femininity are not the best models for their children.

## Q9. AS A WORKING MOTHER I FACE A LOT OF DISTRESS AND DEMANDS – ANY TIPS ON HOW I CAN KEEP STRESS UNDER CONTROL?

Married career women with children are the most stressed group and are even more at risk of an earlier death than single, over-forty, unemployed men. Some of these highly pressurised women complain to me of feeling guilty about coming to hate their children, whose difficult behaviour at critical times can drive them not only to distraction but to beating the uncooperative youngster. These unhappy parents find it reassuring when I point out that it is the difficult behaviour they hate and not the child.

Examples of critical times are mealtimes, bedtimes, going to work and coming home from work. A typical morning scenario sees the young mother under time constraints, trying to get her child washed, dressed, fed and into the child-safety seat in the rear of the car and down to the childminder so that she herself can get to work on time. The toddler is not tuned in to all the needs of his career-mother and, unwittingly, can cause her great distress by downright uncooperative responses to her requests. In desperation, the mother resorts to attempting to control by shouting and sometimes by slapping. Such responses usually result in the child digging in his stubborn heels all the more and this is a contest the mother is highly unlikely to win. Children can be far more resilient in holding out against the attacks of parents.

What is the beleaguered career-mother to do in such trying circumstances? It seems to me that the most important issues she needs to look at are her immediate priorities. When her child is being uncooperative, she is very unlikely to be able to meet all her needs to have the child washed, dressed, fed and seated safely in the car and be on time for the babysitter and work. Surely, in the mornings her priority is to get the child to the babysitter and herself to work? Getting into conflict with the child over eating all his break- fast or brushing his teeth or sitting in the child-safety seat is only going to jeopardise her meeting her own personal needs and, even more distressingly, result in her going to work feeling upset, frustrated and guilty over her loss of control with the child.

The process is not easy but she has a duty to herself and the child to deal with the difficult situation in a positive and cheerful manner. Certainly, she can make a clear and definite request of the child, making sure to be calm and make good and loving eye contact. Children always need to feel that loving them comes before time-keeping, work, hobbies and friends. There is no suggestion here that a working parent should not consider her own needs, but the way the parent communicates and meets such needs is what is in question here. Separateness is the basis for togetherness and each parent needs his or her own separate life that not only enriches individuality but also enriches both the parent-child and the couple's relationship.

When the child does not comply with your request, do not get trapped into nagging or coercing. If it is an issue of dressing, eating, washing teeth and so on, the childminder will have more time to complete these tasks with the child.

If it is a question of getting the child into the car or safety seat, good-humouredly lift the child into the car and into the safety seat, ignoring his protestations. If it is difficult to get him into the safety seat because of his struggling responses, then leave it and set about your priority of getting to the childminder and to work on time. During the journey to the childminder, when the child who has not cooperated with attempts to make contact, let him know cheerfully that you will talk to him when he sits in the safety seat and not until then.

When you arrive at the childminder's home and are leaving the child with her, be sure to give your child a warm hug and say how much you are looking forward to seeing him later. It is important not to carry the conflict into other areas of the child's life.

Equally, when you pick him up later in the day, do not bring up his earlier uncooperativeness. The more the parent works at all times in closeness with a child, the more likely she will gain the cooperation she needs.

When a child's behaviour proves challenging, finding time for creative problem-solving is a necessary step in the resolution process. Enlisting the cooperation of your partner is a good idea, provided he will remain positive and patient with the child. Getting up that bit earlier may help; raising the height of the safety seat in the car so that the child can see out and having your own breakfast first are other possibilities. It is important not to give up the search for positive solutions.

## Q10. SURELY BOYS HAVE TO BE REARED IN A DIFFERENT WAY TO GIRLS?

The belief that males have certain innate capabilities different to females became a basis for social, political and religious engineering that caused, and continues to cause, in less developed countries, major exploitation and marginalisation of females. For example, twenty years ago in Ireland it was assumed that girls did not have the head for mathematics, science and leadership. However, since girls have been given the educational opportunities to study what were traditionally male school subjects, girls outshine males across all subjects. It would seem then that the belief in genetic differences in capabilities between males and females is not substantiated where equal social and educational opportunities are created for males and females. As equal opportunities are extended into political, social, occupational and religious spheres I have no doubt that the advantage that girls are showing in the educational sphere will exhibit itself in these areas as well.

Nonetheless, the notion that 'boys will be boys' and 'girls will be girls' has not bitten the dust, in spite of the narrowing of the gap between behaviours that typically separated the men from the women.

To be fair, there is a small percentage of men who show excellence in areas of knowledge and skill that were traditionally bastions of female power – domestic science, parenting, emotional literacy, nurturance. Not that that is something new – the poets that touched our hearts have been mainly male; renowned chefs are more often than not male and the great psychological innovators have been male.

So what is all this continuing controversy about genetic differences in potential between males and females and how come it is only males who are still bringing it up as an issue? Is it because the notion of genetic difference has served men better than women? Is it a defensive reaction on the part of some males to the growing equality that women are attaining across the full spectrum of human potential? Is it because women are not only holding on to what were their dominant social roles, but are also excelling over men in what were men's dominant social roles? Is it because women are blowing the whistle on unequal and unhappy relationships? Is it because many women are choosing not to marry or to be single parents? Whatever it is, what needs to be seen is that gender was never meant to be seen as something that limited human potential: its purpose was to ensure the survival of the human species. Regrettably, it became a sinister means of employing a genetic issue as a tool for social, educational, political and religious engineering, which now in the more developed countries of the world is being usurped by women and men who are mature and progressive in their thinking.

There are some authors who only say that males and females have equal human potential because they feel that it is the 'politically correct' thing to say. This is just another defensive ploy by threatened males to weaken the emerging reality of equality between men and women.

The question is no longer one of differences in genetic potential between males and females, since the same vast potential for human expansiveness exists in all human beings. The difference comes down, not to gender, but to individuality and choice. Alongside each human being possessing vast potential there is an innate drive in each of us to express our own inherent individuality, uniqueness and giftedness. Whether you are male or female, you have the right to express yourself in any way that fits for you, once your ways do not threaten the presence of other people in your life.

Rather than 'boys being boys' or 'girls being girls', what is needed is for both boys and girls to be human and for each of them as individuals to express and explore the limitless expansiveness of being human, each in his or her own unique way. It is for parents and teachers to encourage the individuality of each child and to create equal opportunities for both sexes to explore their vast potential and unique giftedness.

It is no longer acceptable for males to castigate other males for being different to what has been considered the norm for being male, nor for females to condemn women who do not conform to stereotypical female roles. What is required is the acceptance of each person, male and female, to live out their lives in their own unique ways.

The reality of equality in potential and the human drive to individualise self are major challenges for social systems that heretofore marginalised women, and, it has to be said, confined males in many ways as well. No longer can social systems rely on fitting people into neat packages of male and female. Furthermore, social systems need to reflect on the damage that has been perpetrated based on a very dubious genetic hypothesis, which is now shown to be totally untenable.

## Q11. DO YOU THINK GRANDPARENTS CAN BE OVER-INTERFERING IN THE REARING OF CHILDREN?

Establishing the integrity of the family unit is an important part of parenting. A family needs to have a clear boundary around it that indicates 'we are a family unit, and that largely determines who we are, what we do and who we allow to cross the family threshold'.

It is important that this boundary is not too rigid, as a family needs advice, information, support and help from outsiders. However, the initiative for outside influence must come from within the family.

To tell a family what to do and how to be is a gross invasion of a family's privacy. Even when there are signs of unhappiness and neglect – while it is good that outsiders express concern and offer help – it is not wise to give unsolicited advice.

However, if after such concern is shown children continue to be neglected, then this concern should now be expressed to an agency that can take action to stop the neglect, encourage responsibility and provide the professional help that may be required to bring about desirable change.

Leaving such situations aside, the issue here is the undue influence on the family by outsiders – people who may exert a powerful negative influence on the functioning of the family, who may undermine a couple's relationship and block the self-esteem of family members. The people who most commonly interfere with families are in-laws (living within or outside the family), relatives, neighbours, friends and childminders.

The live-in grandparents or the live-in in-laws are typical sources of negative influences on the family. These 'outsiders' may tell a young mother what to do and what not to do; they may expect her to be there at all times for them; they may interfere with the rearing of the children and they may weaken the couple's relationship.

I have worked with women who, on marrying, moved in with their in-laws and felt that they had no say in the running of the home. It is not wise, even when in-laws are positive and independent, to try to establish a new family under the roof of an existing family. It is a confusing three-generation situation, wherein the self-esteem of all can easily be undermined.

Birds need to fly the nest and build their own nests. A young couple needs to have their own physical space to give them any chance of setting up an independent couple and family life. In a three-generation household the issue of 'who does what' can become a major source of contention.

Privacy is more important that property, and the chant that 'the house will be yours when we're gone' must not sway a young couple from finding their own space. The parents or in-laws may live another thirty or forty years, and a young couple must not postpone their right to independence for any length of time, never mind for so many years.

It is good for a young couple to remember that their parents survived without them before they were born. Furthermore, protection of parents who are healthy and active only blocks their self-esteem and maintains their dependence – hardly an act of caring.

Similarly, parents or in-laws outside the home can exert negative influences. I have worked with women whose mothers or mothers-in-law have a key to the young couple's family home and come and go as they please. This is not acceptable behaviour and the young couple need to assert their right to privacy and to be consulted before visits.

There are parents who expect their married sons or daughters to be on hand whenever they need them. There is no consideration of whether or not it is convenient to do what is being ordered. Of course, I would want to respond to a parent's request, but I would also like to be able to say 'no' when other priorities need my attention without creating an emotional storm. Moreover, the young couple needs to establish that commitments to themselves and their own children take priority.

Neighbours, aunts, uncles, friends and childminders can also be a major influence on family dynamics. There are parents who have great difficulty in saying 'no' to these people and they allow them to rule their couple lives, boss their children and invade their home as they please. These families are then too open to outside influences, so that children become confused, parents feel helpless and no sense of family unity and harmony is present.

Work can also unduly influence the family. The parent whose career takes up most of his or her free time neglects self, the couple relationship and the family. I have worked with many men who, later on in life, regretted not having spent time with their spouses and children. They have often felt hurt when their children as adults did not maintain contact, but the poor contact reflects what they gave to their sons and daughters when they were children. 'As you sow, so shall you reap.'

The task is clear: a young couple must ensure that outsiders or work or study do not lead to the neglect of family welfare or a loss of separateness as a family unit. In clear, firm and positive ways, those who attempt to interfere must be told in no uncertain terms that – while they are loved and welcome in the home – they are in no way to interfere with the functioning of the family.

When parents neglect these responsibilities, they neglect themselves and the family, and this results in a confusing, leaderless and unhappy family.

## Q12. WHAT IS REQUIRED FOR HAPPY FAMILIES?

Happiness is not a state of constant wellbeing but a being in touch with what is happening, whether that be a joyful or distressing experience. Conflict is central to the development of wellbeing in all relationships, and once the conflicting parties are in a place of readiness to look at the reasons behind the conflict, to take due responsibility and to follow through in action, then stability will be restored and deepened. This is true for all relationships, be it friend and friend, partner and partner, parent and child, child and child, worker and employer, and so on. However, for a mature response to conflict to occur, each party to the conflict needs to be in a relatively good place of personal security and independence. It is highly unlikely that a parent who has to be always right will listen to the other person's side of the story. Similarly, a child who is frightened of a parent is unlikely to open up to that parent on the hidden reasons for his difficult behaviour.

Personal maturity is the measure of an individual's own relationship with self. When individuals are disconnected from some or all aspects of self, they are not in a place of inner solidity to embrace conflict as a route to furthering the wellbeing of a relationship. On the contrary, the conflict poses a considerable threat to those who doubt their own inner worth and capability, and the response will be an escalation of defensive behaviour rather than an openness to understanding and resolving the conflict issues. Unless these parents embrace their inner conflicts they are not in a place to resolve outer conflicts. Next to loving children, the effective resolution of the inevitable conflicts that arise in a family is paramount to family wellbeing.

It would appear from the foregoing that there are three main characteristics to the establishment of a mature relationship within or outside the family:

- a solid and enduring relationship with self
- a supportive relationship with others, whether adult or child
- the embracing of conflict as a passport to deepening the quality of the relationship.

The good news is that recent Irish research has produced evidence to support what common sense and clinical practice have long heralded as being the keys to family wellbeing. This study, as mentioned earlier, was commissioned by the Ceifin Centre, Burren, Co. Clare. The main findings are in line with the characteristics of a mature family given above: a child's wellbeing largely depends on each parent's psychological and physical wellbeing, her or his supportiveness as a parent and skills in resolving conflicts.

In the study, family relationships emerged as the crucial influence. An important aspect of relating was resolving difficulties in the family as they arose, be they about household chores, pocket money, choice of friends or schoolwork. Major distress continued in families where problems went unresolved.

What the study also showed was that family type or material wealth are not significant issues. The finding on family type is significant, as in the New Ireland there are many different family types compared to the traditional family. What the study reveals is that it is the quality of relating that counts, not the issue of lone-parenting or separated parenting or same-sex parenting. Given the high rate of marital separation, the study also emphasised the significance and positive influence of the non-resident father who maintains closeness with his children. Marital breakdown does not have to mean family breakdown, and separated parents have a responsibility not to carry their conflicts into the separation and to ensure that the father is given reasonable opportunities to maintain a close relationship with his children.

It has been often said that the cause of all human problems is a lack of loving. The Clare study supports this truism.

# CHAPTER THREE

# WHAT ARE THE SKILLS NEEDED FOR EVERYDAY PARENTING?

- □ INTRODUCTION
- □ SPECIFIC QUESTIONS
    - Q1. Isn't it enough that we show love to our children?
    - Q2. How important is it to hug a child?
    - Q3. I treat all the children the same: no harm in that, is there?
    - Q4. How can I best create emotional security for my child?
    - Q5. How can I help my child to 'just do it' and not be tentative, timid and unsure?
    - Q6. How does non-verbal communication influence how I relate to my children?
    - Q7. No matter what I say to my children, it doesn't seem to have any effect. What am I doing wrong?
    - Q8. How can I best communicate with my child?
    - Q9. What are the integral rights of children?
    - Q10. How can I best encourage my child to take on new challenges?
    - Q11. Have we forgotten how being belittled as children had a devastating effect on us? It appears we have, because some of us repeat the belittling. Why?
    - Q12. Isn't it true that a good spanking never does a child any harm?
    - Q13. How can I identify when my child is troubled?
    - Q14. If children learn so much through observation, is there any need to spend time on training them to acquire certain skills?

Q15. My child is adamant that 'I can do it myself', but I feel he should accept my help. What do you suggest?

Q16. Should children be paid to do chores?

Q17. Is it important that children experience aloneness?

Q18. Children deserve to be given toys, don't they?

Q19. How can I best discipline children's difficult behaviours?

Q20. What is the best way of dealing with bullying?

Q21. How is television viewing best managed in a family?

## INTRODUCTION

Knowing the broad strokes of parenting outlined in the last chapter is an essential backdrop to developing the specific skills that are required for the day-to-day rearing of children.

Skills development needs to focus closely on the physical, emotional, intellectual, educational, social, behavioural and creative needs of children and how best to respond to those needs. Parents can often get into conflict with children around food, and mealtimes can become a constant battle and a seriously unhappy time for both parents and children.

Helping children to identify and express their feelings is a crucial parenting skill. Sadly, many male children appear to be deprived of the opportunities to become emotionally literate. Suicide and aggression among young men have often got to do with the repression or suppression of their inner feelings. Mothers, who still do 90 per cent of the parenting, often unwittingly steer male children away from the feminine responsibilities within the family. This results in male children not learning how to identify their own feelings or respond to feelings in others. 'Big boys don't cry' is still a reality. Along with that is the more serious issue of male children not developing their feminine side, which has got to do with the expression of love, tenderness, kindness, empathy, compassion and provision of nurturance for self and others. On the other hand, female children are guided down the femininity route and away from the realisation of their masculine side. Much of what is good in the world has got to do with the presence of the masculine qualities of drive, ambition, taking power, decisiveness, order, invention, assertion and definitiveness. Similarly, much of what is good in the world is owing to the feminine qualities outlined above. It is the wise parent who seeks to realise both sides of her children's humanity. However, she cannot do that unless she herself stands solidly on the foot of masculinity and on the foot of femininity.

How best to create a safe and dynamic learning environment for children (see also Chapter Six) is another requirement of parents. Any criticism and hurt around learning can have long-lasting effects on how children view themselves intellectually and how they approach learning.

Infants and toddlers love to learn, are eager to learn, are fearless, adventurous and spontaneous. Nonetheless, when you ask adults about their approach to learning, the response 99 per cent of the time is 'I dread failure' or 'Success is what counts' or 'You're best to keep your head down and go for the average'. Fear of failure, fear of success or addiction to success are common among adults. What is even more worrying is the enmeshment of self with knowledge and skills, so that adults feel that what they do determines their worth in this world. This is a frightening situation because no behaviour defines the worth of any adult or any child. Furthermore, education, age, job, status, wealth or fame are not indices of maturity or wisdom. If parents want their children to enjoy the whole adventure of learning and education, they need first to recover their own original love, eagerness and fearlessness around learning.

Children need to develop a whole range of behavioural skills in order to take responsibility for their *own* lives, the latter being the ultimate aim of parenting. Children have immense potential to be 'response-able' and it is the parent's responsibility to create as many opportunities as possible for each child to actualise that potential. Children are very clever and they let parents know very strongly their need to be 'response-able' by declaring frequently 'I want to do it myself'. Parents need to respond positively to that declaration and be sure that they do not do for children what children can do for themselves. Overprotection of children, particularly male children, has brought about a great helplessness among those children in later life around taking responsibility for their own lives. 'Response-ableness' has to be present before young adults can take responsibility for their own lives. Parents who overprotect children need to seriously look at what it is in them that wants their child to be dependent and helpless.

Discipline is central to behavioural responsibility and parents need all the training they can get to have appropriate and fair discipline practices within the home. Most parents find it difficult to accept that all discipline starts with the parent herself and that the parent who demands of children to act in ways contrary to the parent's own way will not be effective in disciplining difficult behaviour.

Many parents worry about the social development of their children and can experience intense disquiet when their child is introverted or slow to make friends or quick to make enemies. Knowledge of what to watch out for and ways of helping children to make friends is required. Parents would need to look at their own level of social confidence, because a child can identify with that parent and thereby develop similar social reticence as modelled by his parent.

Whether parents like it or not, each child will eventually go the exact opposite to the other children in the family. This creative expression of difference is frequently missed as are other attempts of children to express creativity. When children do not 'fit in' to the expectations of their parents, their unique expression of their creativity goes abegging. The danger here is that the child loses all motivation and settles for a limited and routine existence.

The questions set out below touch on the most important issues raised above.

## Q1. ISN'T IT ENOUGH THAT WE SHOW LOVE TO OUR CHILDREN?

I believe that the prime need of every human being is to be loved and to love. In order to experience both of these aspects of love, we need to learn to love and accept ourselves. This self-regard becomes the basis for the formation of the independent and unconditional giving and receiving of love. The need to love and be loved are inextricably bound together. When partners, friends or parents enter relationships lacking a love of self, they may be unable to either give or receive love.

Infants have been maligned when it comes to giving love. It has been too long assumed that babies and young children are narcissistic (the belief that they are the centre of the universe) and that they do not show love to parents or others. This has not been my experience, and certainly mothers believe that their infants reach out not only to be loved but also to love. However, whether the babies will maintain these two ways of loving will be determined by how the individual parent responds to these expressions of love. When a parent herself has difficulty in receiving love but not giving it, she becomes the 'carer'. On the other hand, when a parent has difficulty in showing love but not in receiving it, he becomes the 'taker'. It is fascinating how stereotyping has led to women having no difficulty in showing love but considerable difficulty in receiving it, while men are good at receiving but poor at showing love. It means then when children reach out to their mothers to love and be loved, but only the latter behaviour gets a response, the children may learn to receive love but not dare show it to these mothers. We have all come across the pheonomenon where any attempt to demonstrate love to a carer is dismissed or causes embarrassment or is diluted by such statements as 'you shouldn't say that' or 'I don't deserve it' or 'you don't really mean it'. Similarly, when children reach out to those fathers who are good receivers but poor givers of love, they learn to show love but not to ask for it for themselves.

Parents and children who cannot show love but can receive it have had to imprison their innate need to show love. It is too risky to exhibit love for fear of losing the permission to receive it. Equally, parents and children who can show but not receive love are cut off from the freedom to ask for love, as this might mean losing the right to show love.

It is the parent with whom the child identifies most who will determine largely whether one or both aspects of loving will perpetuate. Identification is a process whereby the child takes on the ways and characteristics of the parent who represents the greater emotional threat. When parents are comfortable in both giving and receiving love, children's identity formation is far less tied to conforming to parental ways. It grows more from the child's own uniqueness, lovability, vast capability and creativity. When this type of open parenting operates, children develop also a sense of their own goodness, worth, ability, difference and lovability.

This is what self-worth is all about, where the two-sided loving of parents reflects for children their wonder. Children then feel that not only are they worthy enough to receive love but also to give it. However, when the parent with whom the child identifies cannot show love but can receive it, the child will repeat this pattern. When the opposite pattern operates, the child will necessarily and wisely repeat it. In either scenario, children are able to show at least one aspect of loving.

Sadly, there are homes where children's attempts to ask for and show love receive a neutral or harsh and punishing response. Not to be able to show and receive love is tantamount to blowing out the light of a candle; it plunges children into the blackness of despair and helplessness.

When adults or children feel it is only safe to show love, they have deep doubts that they are good enough to receive it. Equally, when adults and children feel it is only safe to receive love, they have deep doubts that they are good enough to give it. Only the double experience of loving frees adults and children to truly love themselves and others.

## Q2. HOW IMPORTANT IS IT TO HUG A CHILD?

The embrace, the hug, the silent holding are the most powerful ways of communicating love and security to children. In adult relationships touch is an important indicator of warmth and affection. In medical and psychological practice touch has long been regarded as healing and, indeed, there has been a whole range of 'touch' therapies developed to help those who are in pain, under stress or emotionally vulnerable. It is a sad state of affairs that parents, teachers, relatives, childminders, nurses and others are now often afraid to spontaneously hug a child or to physically comfort a child who is in distress or who just needs the security and comfort of an adult body. I know of fathers who are nervous of being physically affectionate with their daughters due to the rise in estranged partners accusing their husbands of sexually violating their daughters. Many of these claims are not substantiated and can sometimes be a ploy used in situations of bitter child custody battles. It is also the case that teenage daughters in conflict with their fathers can threaten to or actually accuse them of sexual violations. It would appear that it has become extremely unsafe for men to physically express their love for their children. Women, too, though less threatened, are nervous of physical contact with children. In school, both male and female teachers are warned not to be alone with a child and to refrain from physical contact.

In any physical expression of love and comfort it is the intention that counts and the readiness to respect the physical, sexual and emotional boundaries of the child or adult. When physical contact is between an adult and a child, the adult has the extra responsibility of not crossing children's physical and sexual boundaries. There are times when children do not feel safe enough or are not disposed to physical affection and it is essential that adults respect those boundaries. There are adults who, with the best of intentions, have the idea that children always want to be picked up, hugged or engage in 'horse-play', but the reality is that children, like adults, are not always in that receptive physical place. It is then invasive not to check – children's bodies communicate very quickly when they do not want to be held. The child's body may stiffen, retreat, curl up, battle or protest when physical contact is not welcome.

When children are receptive it would be a profound privation not to give them the demonstration of physical

affection and comfort. As adults, rather than being controlled by media hype on sexual violation and paedophilia, we
need to hold on to what is natural and know that our intention
is to communicate love and not in any way violate children's
physical and sexual boundaries. Not only does taking on the
fear of potential sexual accusations result in a privation for
children, but it is a great loss to adults who can give and
receive so much through their physical contact with children.
Parenting and care of children are self-sacrificing professions
and the physical enjoyment of children would be a severe loss
to those who love, rear and educate children.

It would be naïve of us to believe that there are not times
when some sexual arousal occurs around children, but
arousal does not equal sexual intention, and once the intention
remains honourable then no change in behaviour is necessary. Nobody disputes that the sexual drive is a powerful
biological drive both in adults and in children. All possible
safeguards are required to ensure children's sexual safety,
not only from adults, but from older children as well. But
safeguarding must not lead to a touch taboo.

There is no doubt that we still have a long way to go in
celebrating sexuality and, regrettably, openness on sexual
matters is still taboo in many families, churches and
classrooms. For example, the one subject that 80 per cent of
adolescents do not talk about to their parents is sex. The
more that the sexual taboo disappears, the less likely that
the touch taboo that is emerging will continue.

## Q3. I TREAT ALL THE CHILDREN THE SAME: NO HARM IN THAT, IS THERE?

'I've treated all the children the same' is a response I have
heard from many parents who bring me a child who is

exhibiting distressing behaviours. Another frequent comment is 'I don't understand why this child is a problem and my other children are not presenting any difficulties?'

As regards the first question it is impossible to treat each child the same. Firstly, consider the gender of the child. Typically, parents respond to boys and girls in quite different ways. Observations show that most mothers, who still carry 90 per cent of the parenting, steer their male children away from the feminine qualities of tenderness, nurturance, empathy, expression of feelings and compassion, and steer them steadily into the masculine qualities of taking power, ambition, drive and invention. Girls tend to be reared in the opposite direction to boys. What all children need are the opportunities to develop their limitless potential across the full breadth of human behaviours, including both masculine and feminine qualities.

Whilst gender may explain why one child may be problematic compared to another, what about the situation where all the children are of one gender? One possible and frequently quoted explanation is birth place in the family. Each additional member to a family changes the dynamics of the family and, more often than not, the dynamics of the marital relationship within two-parent families. There is the added difficulty that nowadays anything up to 40 per cent of children only experience a two-parent family set-up up to the age of six to seven years. The effects on children of the marital turmoil, marital breakdown and the continuation of conflict following the separation are well documented, with the older children tending to suffer more. Some of these children who are traumatised by the conflict between their parents often say to me 'Why did they part, they were fighting before they parted and they're fighting since they parted?' A good question! For the sake of their children and, indeed, for the sake of themselves, separated parents need to draw closure on conflict and be available to nurture and support their children and support each other in that process.

The middle child in a family is often seen as the one who is more likely to prove difficult, as he may be sandwiched between a jealous older sibling and a younger 'favoured' sibling. However, vigilant parents, who notice the early signs of insecurity in any one of their children, will take the necessary steps to help the child who feels threatened by their attention to the other children. However, when the parents fail to observe and act on the particular child's insecurity, then the child's place in the family may be voiced as the cause of the child's disturbance. But, if truth be told, the deeper reason lies in a deficit in parenting.

What is often not appreciated is that a parent interacts with each child differently and that it can be truly said that each child has a different parent. It cannot be any other way; each parent is a unique individual and each child is unique. When two unique persons get together, the interactions and the relationship that develops can only be of a unique nature. There is the added issue that each parent carries emotional baggage from their earlier experiences into their roles of partners and parents, and, quite subconsciously, will project aspects of that immaturity onto each child in a different way. For example, a parent who, as the eldest child in her family of origin, was made to take on adult responsibilities for both parents and younger siblings, may unwittingly overcompensate with the first child by overprotecting him or her from having to take on any responsibilities. One must also be aware that a child observes family dynamics very carefully and decides on unique ways he can express his individuality and draw attention to himself. He will also determine quite early on which parent most favours him and will form a coalition with that parent. It is for these reasons that each child actively goes opposite to a sibling in the expression of his individuality and, inevitably, this individualising pattern draws unique responses both from parents and from fellow siblings. When parents marvel at how a child manifests himself in such an individual way, the child will feel secure in his individuation; the contrary is also true.

Proof of the above phenomena comes from the totally different reminiscences that are related by the adult children of one family. You would swear that each member had a different family, and the truth is, each did.

## Q4. HOW CAN I BEST CREATE EMOTIONAL SECURITY FOR MY CHILD?

Parents tend to be acutely aware of the physical dangers that may threaten their children's wellbeing. They erect barriers at the top and bottom of stairways, ensure that gateways at fronts and backs of houses are securely fastened, remove sharp objects, medications, etc., from children's reach – all in loving efforts to minimise threats to their children's physical welfare. Later on, when children are at a school-going age, they are taught the safety code for crossing roads, are warned not to talk to or take lifts from strangers and to avoid certain areas of town.

What often goes unrecognised by parents are the more threatening emotional perils that children encounter daily. Unless these dangers are removed or minimised or children are taught how to cope with such stressful events, the door to their emotional development may be partially or, sometimes, firmly closed.

Examples of these risks to children's emotional wellbeing are:

□ Not measuring up to parents' expectations
□ Telling the truth
□ Taking on new challenges
□ Establishing a new friendship
□ Starting school
□ Encountering mistakes and failures

In taking on these tasks and experiences the child may worry:

□ Will I be loved?
□ Will I be punished?
□ Will I be successful?
□ Will I be liked?
□ Will I cope?
□ Will I be crtiticised?

Unwittingly, parents' own expectations of and reactions to children pose the greatest threats to their children's emotional security. When expectations are unrealistic, when children are pushed into challenges that spring from parents' own regrets about their childhoods and also from the dangerous assumption that their children are photocopies of them, the risk of 'not being good enough' hangs like the Sword of Damocles over children's heads. It is wise for parents to realise that each child is unique and has a strong inner drive to establish his or her own individuality and distinct way of being in this world. To miss out on this fact is to doom children to living the lives of parents and others rather than living their own lives. Emphasis on academic performance, comparisons with other siblings, making too much of success and belittling failure are further blocks to children's emotional development.

All of the above ways of relating to children result frequently in a tide of ridicule, scoldings, 'put-down' messages, cynicism, sarcasm, physical punishment, hostile silences, unfairness and injustice. Children seldom emerge unscathed from the scars of these threats, and it takes considerable healing efforts when they are adults to change how they see and feel about themselves.

It is not that parents ever deliberately create emotional uncertainty and insecurity for their children, but parents' own vulnerability and dependence on others lead them to behave towards their children in the same punishing way they are with themselves. These parents see their children as extensions of themselves and any falling short or failure (and, indeed, success) on the children's part are seen as reflections on the parents. It is a case of parent heal yourself before you can effectively provide emotional safety for children. Clearly, insecurity runs on a continuum: the greater the vulnerability of parents, the greater the emotional risks to children and vice versa.

The creation of emotional safety in the home is paramount for children. In loving and accepting themselves, in becoming independent of the judgement of others and of success and failure, parents can provide an environment that helps children develop a realistic sense of themselves. It follows then that there needs to be an absence of criticism, ridicule, scoldings, comparisons, cynicism, sarcasm, hostile silences, and the presence of unconditional love, warmth, compassion, understanding, encouragement, humour, belief in, acceptance and support. All of us lose control at times with children, but once you genuinely and sincerely apologise, the unsafety created can be quickly extinguished.

Not all the threats to children's emotional security reside in the home. However, when the home provides secure and safe relationships, the child is better equipped to deal with the uncertainties and threats that arise in the outside world.

Parents can also teach their children either before or after threatening eventualities how to understand and cope. They can sit down with their child and go through the things that might happen when she takes on a new challenge, for instance initiating a friendship. The other child may say 'no', tease her or be sarcastic. Help your child to hold on to her own good sense of self and to the realisation that the other child's behaviour is about him and not even remotely about her. When it is a situation occurring after the fact and your child is feeling hurt, then listening and comforting her are the first responses to show and, later on, when the child is emotionally ready to listen, you can help her to regain her sense of self and to stay separate from the judgements of others. Most of all, your child needs to know that no matter what happens outside (and inside) the home – not bringing home the perfect school report, or not being selected for the school team, or not managing to initiate or maintain a friendship – in your eyes she is always loved and wanted. The child is vastly more important than a particular achievement that is here today and gone tomorrow.

## Q5. HOW CAN I HELP MY CHILD TO 'JUST DO IT' AND NOT BE TENTATIVE, TIMID AND UNSURE?

A young woman who has attained excellence in an array of career and artistic endeavours remembers being told frequently by her father whenever she voiced wanting to take on a new challenge to 'just do it'. There was no question that she had to get it right or be the best or compete with others; no, the encouragement was to take on the challenge as an adventure, not as a test or trial. Not surprisingly, as a young adult she continues to benefit from her father's wisdom and is not one bit shy of risk-taking.

Risk-taking is crucial to advancing one's knowledge of self, others and the world. There are 10 per cent of elderly people who cannot be distinguished from younger people in terms of physical fitness, mental agility, creativity and productivity. What makes this group of elderly people stand out from their peers is that they have continuously challenged themselves across several areas of living during their long lives.

Toddlers tend to 'just do it', but quickly they pick up on either the impatience, crossness, irritability or anxiety a parent shows when they risk-take. Because toddlers know they depend on their parents for all aspects of their well-being, they conform to the restrictions imposed on them and, sadly, depending on the frequency and intensity of the blocks to their risk-taking, the door to 'just doing it' either partially or solidly closes.

It is not that parents or teachers or other significant adults in children's lives deliberately block a child's progress, but the adults' own blocking experiences when they were children are now repeated with their own children. Unless adults reflect on their experiences around curiosity, learning and risk-taking as children and attempt to free their imprisoned adventurous spirit, they are not in a position to inspire children to retain their eagerness to learn. Parents and teachers can only bring children to the same level of love of learning and excitement that they have retained themselves.

Parents need to be wary of confusing love of learning with addiction to success and perfectionism. Those who see learning as an adventure are driven by an innate love of learning; those who are perfectionistic and dependent on success are driven by fears of failure, rejection and criticism. Furthermore, the latter group will only take risks in areas of endeavour where they feel they will excel, while the former group tend to be 'all-rounders' and enjoy risk-taking across the full spectrum of human behaviour.

There is a sad statistic that approximately 80 per cent of students and adults 'go for the average'. This group shows limited initiative and productivity, not because they have not got the potential to be expansive in their living, but because less hurt and humiliation are experienced when you convince people 'I'm your average person'.

The person who 'just does it' lives life from the inside-out; the person who has learnt to avoid or limit risk-taking lives life from the outside-in. It is not too difficult to determine which group you are in. Check what you do when opportunities come up to speak your mind, to express a new idea, to demonstrate initiative, to have a different viewpoint to the majority, to see things differently to your parent or boss, to change career, to express difficulties in a primary relationship and so on. Not easy, is it? But you are here to live your own life and your spirit will continue to throw opportunities in your way to liberate you from your fears. The more support we have for risk-taking, the easier it is to take up the gauntlet.

It is a hopeful sign that there are some work organisations that encourage and reward their workers to 'just do it' if they feel some idea might benefit the company. The emphasis is on the risk-taking and not on the result; this is wise, as focusing on results fosters performance anxiety, which quickly dries up the well of risk-taking and the love of learning and work. Homes and schools would do well to take inspiration from such work settings and restore the adventure of living to those children who have lost it. However, such a transformation is only likely to occur when parents and teachers rekindle their risk-taking spirits.

## Q6. HOW DOES NON-VERBAL COMMUNICATION INFLUENCE HOW I RELATE TO MY CHILDREN?

Non-verbal communication accounts for 80 per cent of the messages we send to others. Facial expression, tone of voice, body posture, nature of eye contact (for example, intense stare, fleeting glance, benign look), voice volume, physical gestures (for example, finger wagging, waving clenched fist, dismissive wave) – these are all examples of this level of communication. For communication to be effective it is essential that the non-verbal messages are saying the same thing as the verbal communication, otherwise the child will respond to the non-verbal message. For instance, when a parent says to a child, 'Michael, I want you to put your toys away now', but there is no firmness in her tone of voice, it is likely the child will continue to play with his toys.

Compared to adults, children are far more in tune with non-verbal communication, a skill that adults tend to lose as they grow older. Children's first language is non-verbal: in the first year or two they get many of their needs met by communicating through their bodies and by different kinds of crying and other noises. Also they are experts at reading their parents' faces and detecting differences in their parents' tone of voice and body posture.

Unwittingly, parents frequently trigger difficult behaviour on the part of children because of the tone they use. Take the following example, when the tone of voice conveys quite a different message to the actual words spoken:

> Sara's mother was helping her with her homework. Sara was struggling to understand what she was supposed to do. In exasperation and with more than a hint of impatience in her voice, the mother says, 'Well surely you understand something?' Sara's response was to look even more perplexed and bury her head in the book.

Sara's mother's tone of voice indicated that she had little belief in Sara's ability to understand her homework. Belief is central to a child's retention of a love of learning and a natural curiosity. In the above scene, the mother's impatient tone of voice added considerably to the child's rising discouragement and Sara was quick to spot this and she responded appropriately.

It is very noticeable that adults rarely talk to children in the normal tone they use to talk to each other. The simpering 'baby talk' and the condescending 'simple talk' which parents and other adults use with young children always results in children feeling inferior. The manner, body posture, facial expression and tone of voice that parents use when speaking to children would never be used with another adult.

Parents need to make it a practice to listen to and observe themselves in the company of children, and to begin to notice how, unwittingly, they demonstrate disrespect to their children. Parents are prone to talk down to children, to exhibit false gaiety and go over the top to get a response from children or talk to children with saccharine sweetness to gain cooperation. Such behaviours are opportunities for parents to reflect on what is their basic concept of parenting and to what degree they may be projecting some of their own insecurities and fears onto children.

When parents are dependent on their children liking them, their communication often lacks firmness. Also, if a parent has a fear in asserting her rights and needs in her marriage and other relationships, she may carry this anxiety into her relationship with her child. Similarly, when a parent compensates for inner insecurity through dominating others, he is likely to do the same with his child. The challenge for both of these parents is to realise their unique worthiness and to communicate out from that solid interior place.

It is only when parents are on a solid footing inside of themselves that they can relate to their children as friends, on an equal footing with them, and communicate both verbally and non-verbally in direct and clear ways.

## Q7. NO MATTER WHAT I SAY TO MY CHILDREN, IT DOESN'T SEEM TO HAVE ANY EFFECT. WHAT AM I DOING WRONG?

There are several ways in which a parent's words cease to matter to a child, the most common being a parent not following through on what she says. Threatening children with unrealistic sanctions such as 'I'll kill you if I catch you playing ball on the road' will not be successful with children, as they know full well you cannot follow through with such a threat. When stating a consequence to an irresponsible behaviour, parents need to ensure that the sanction is something they can follow through on, like deprivation of a privilege. Stating *specifically* the response to a difficult behaviour is crucial, so that when the child does not respond to a reasonable request you can follow through with the talked-about sanction. Actions always speak louder than words when parents are attempting to establish boundaries and limitations that provide children with a sense of security.

Parents cannot possibly expect their parenting methods to be effective if they apply them inconsistently and haphazardly. Children have no sense of what is required by parents when they do not make their words matter. Children deserve and require consistency of behaviour on the part of their parents and other significant adults in order for them to feel secure. They also learn to be responsible for themselves.

To provide children with the desired security and opportunities to assume responsibility that they deserve, it is important that parents make their words matter in situations such as the following:

- Giving children choice
- Meeting their own needs
- Rising in the morning
- Responsibility for pets

This list is by no means exhaustive, but if a parent is consistent in following through on these daily childhood responsibilities, it is likely that her behaviour will generalise to other areas.

Allowing children to choose is the bedrock of the skill of decision-making, which will determine how wisely they make choices on all aspects of living. Children who are told what to do, say, feel and think lack this essential life-skill and struggle with adult challenges. Equally, children who are over-protected, whereby most things are done for them, as adults feel helpless in the face of adult responsibilities. Only those children who are given opportunities and encouraged to make choices will cope with the endless decisions that adolescent and adult life entails. Children need to be allowed to make mistakes; they learn mostly through experience, not from parents' sermons or cajoling them into their ways. It is important when children are given choice on what to wear, tidying up, friendships, what to do in their free time, etc., that parents do not have a hidden agenda or do not attempt to persuade them into agreement with them. Consistency and keeping your word are what matters here.

Giving children a weekly allowance is another way of providing an opportunity for them to practise wise decision-making. It is a familiar experience of parents to endure children's 'I want, I want, I want', but saying 'use your allowance money' teaches a child how to value her pocket-money more. Giving into a child's demands or allowing her to borrow against next week's allowance is not recommended.

Provision of an alarm clock is the way of handing over responsibility to children for getting themselves up in the morning. Parents need to desist from the tendency to 'make' children get up, as this, once again, means that the parent is not following through on her word. When a parent sets this opportunity up for a child, she needs to be in a position herself to be able to follow through when the child fails to respond to the alarm clock. When a parent is in the position where she has to be at her job, she needs to be able to hand over responsibility to her partner or childminder to bring the children to school late. Remember, children learn best through experience. Giving responsibility to the children has to be carried through day after day with no leniency; otherwise children have a loophole that they can exploit at will.

Another area of child responsibility that frequently falls back on the mother is the care of a pet. A child will promise anything to have the pet, but many parents know only too well how the novelty wears off and the feeding and caring for the pet are quickly neglected. Before getting a pet, the parent needs to sit down with the child and discuss the responsibility and what is to be done when these responsibilities are neglected. A good question to ask the child is 'How many times can neglect be permitted?' When the child names a number, and it is reasonable, the parent needs to add 'And you agree that when you neglect your responsibility that number of times, we will then have to return the pet?' Parents have a responsibility to follow through and place the pet elsewhere; they do their children no favour by supporting neglect.

## Q8. HOW CAN I BEST COMMUNICATE WITH MY CHILD?

Talking with children is an important part of parenting and it is not a skill that parents automatically possess. Indeed, many parents talk *to* children – albeit in a friendly way – but nonetheless what the child experiences is a sermon. There are some parents who talk *at* children and children experience this as threatening to their having any voice of their own. Talking to or at children involves telling them what to think, say and do; it expresses a demand for obedience and expects them to conform to how the parent sees the world. Talking *with* children involves the parent and the child looking at ideas together and problem-solving together.

Communication difficulties between parents and children come to a head during the teenage years, and the earlier patterns of family communication will largely determine the extent of the communication problem. Central to effective communication is the parent's ability to respect the child, even when the parent disagrees with the child.

Parents would do well to remember that a child has a mind of his own and any attempt to impose their mind on the child is always counter-productive. This is not to say that parents do not have the right to influence their children, but influencing and forcing are very different experiences. Influencing is where the parents express their own views, beliefs, needs and preferences as a message about themselves; controlling or forcing is where the parents attempt to impose their ways on children.

Each child is a unique powerful, creation, and is always an active participant in the development of his or her personality.

Parents need to be willing to accept that there is more than one point of view – that their way of viewing matters is not the only way. Finding out what children think about situations is not difficult because young children are so very free in expressing themselves. However, if parents are impatient, irritable or cross, or if they find fault with what children think, then children quickly learn not to expose themselves to such threatening experiences. And slowly but surely parents inadvertently close the door to inter-communication.

If, on the other hand, parents spontaneously listen and value a child's ideas, examine them with her, explore with her the possible outcomes, ask questions like 'What do you feel might happen?'; 'How will you feel afterwards?'; 'What do you think the other person will feel?' then the child will discover a sense of her parents being interested in her ideas and being willing to help her solve her life difficulties.

One of the major blocks to effective communication is the notion that parents always know 'what is right' for their children. This creates a superiority on the parent's part and inequality in the relationships. It also prevents the child finding out for himself the usefulness of his ideas. In any case, it is inaccurate to say a child's ideas are 'wrong'. Parents also risk the response of the child clamming up. Furthermore, telling a child 'you're wrong' is an example of talking *at* a child.

'Jane, you know it is wrong to hit your sister. Shame on you. You know you must love and be kind to your sister. After all, you are her big sister.' Such a moralising response is an example of talking *to* a child and it provides no opportunity for the child to express what has led to the aggression and how she can learn from it. Talking *with* the child involves asking 'Jane, I would like to know what led you to hit your sister?' 'She keeps getting in my way, what else could I do but push her out of the way?' 'Well I hear your frustration, but how about looking at other ways of dealing with your sister's difficult behaviour?' A discussion is now possible as

the what and why of Jane's behaviour have been acknowledged.

Parents need to be open to admitting that there is more
than one viewpoint – that their way of seeing things is not
the only way. Certainly, parents need to be sensitive to the
child's self-esteem when they discover that their child views
things differently. If parents say anything that puts the child
down or embarrasses or humiliates him or causes him to lose
face, then healthy communication has ceased.

Certainly, a parent can say 'I see it differently but you have
the right to see things your way. Let's watch and see how
things work out'. This response equalises the situation, and
progress in communication is likely to ensue. If parents wish for
their children to broaden their viewpoints, they need to create
the opportunities for them to see that another way might
work better. Most of all, they need to include their children as
partners in the difficult task of creating family harmony.

Many parents have the idea that the 'new psychological way'
of communicating with children is giving in to children and
giving up on parental leadership. On the contrary, true leadership involves talking *with* children and providing opportunities for them to take charge of themselves. Cooperation is
much more likely to emerge in such a family.

## Q9. WHAT ARE THE INTEGRAL RIGHTS OF CHILDREN?

It is interesting how quickly we have forgotten that, in the
not too distant past, the physical punishment of children
was part and parcel of rearing children, and caning in school
and church were seen as 'educative'. Furthermore, only quite
recently has it been acknowledged that children have equal
rights to adults, that they deserve respect, positive parenting
and teaching and to be free of physical, sexual and

emotional violations. The individuality, creativity and rich emotional lives of children and how they perceive self, others and the world are only beginning to be recognised and explored.

There are still remnants of the time when children were seen as little adults who required no special care and could be sent up chimneys, down mines and to care for babies and adults in need. The notion that children are the possessions of parents and teachers, to be moulded to match adults' needs, is still alive and well. But, the idea that children should be seen and not heard has faded and there is no doubt that children's needs are now seen as significant.

The persistent neglect of children was widespread not too long ago. When people throw up their hands in horror on hearing or reading of the physical, sexual and emotional abuse of children, they are blinding themselves to what was an everyday reality for many children. Whilst considerable progress has been made in reducing the physical and sexual violation of children, as a society we have not yet come to the maturity of seeing that *emotional* hurting is still a pervasive experience for both adults and children. Impatience, irritability, bullying, cynicism, sarcasm, hostile humour, dismissiveness and aggression mark many interactions between adults and adults, adults and children, and children and children.

All physical, sexual and emotional neglect of children is on a continuum from mild to severe, but, somehow, when we read or see of mothers or fathers physically hurting or torturing or murdering babies or the discovery of paedophile rings, we do not want these realities to be true or we condemn the adults who perpetrate such abhorrence as 'evil', 'bad', 'deviant', or 'insane'. To face these horrors of children being tortured or sexually violated means having to face a whole set of beliefs and ideas we possess about those adults who have responsibilities for children. Our strongest belief is that adults are naturally protective towards children. However, the neglectful ways of rearing and educating children in the not too distant past blows that notion out of the water. Furthermore, even in a time of more 'enlightened' child-rearing practices, every parent can experience great love towards a child one minute and an overwhelming rage, frustration and even hate the next minute. Thankfully, more and more adults perceive the latter feelings as being more about their own blocked needs and they take action for themselves rather than taking their frustrations out on children. However, let us be honest; at times we all lose control with children, but at least we can apologise and attempt to heal the rift in the relationship and the child's self-esteem as soon as possible.

Is there a way that we can understand and absorb the more serious neglect of children and find compassion in our hearts for those who perpetrate such horrors? Judgement, con-demnation, shouting for their blood, does not make us much different to those who have perpetrated such dark needs. There is evidence that women who injure their children do so in order to receive attention, concern and compassion for themselves. It is not that these women consciously plan the hurting of their children to get attention, but rather that they learnt when they were children themselves that the only attention given to them was when they were sick or showing signs of distress. Clinical evidence shows that some of these mothers were victims of physical and sexual brutality when they were children and that kindness towards them came from the concern of others. They were used by their mothers or fathers to manifest the neglect that they, in turn, had experienced in childhood, the hope being that the emptiness inside of them would be seen by others. When children are violated, it is highly dangerous for them to voice the violations, and so the mind is forced, unconsciously, to find other ways to bring the horrors experienced to the light of day.

The challenge for others is to see that adults who physically and sexually violate children do not do so from the perspective of absolute cruelty. They do not set out to pervert relationship; it is more that they are unconsciously manifesting the cruelty, abuse, neglect and exploitation they encountered in their childhood years.

## Q10. HOW CAN I BEST ENCOURAGE MY CHILD TO TAKE ON NEW CHALLENGES?

Courage is the essence of the heart (*cœur* – the heart). We all need courage at certain times, and we can be supported by the en-couragement of others along life's path. When there is no encouragement, then it feels like there is no love, and we experience discouragement. Genuine encouragement is one of the greatest gifts we can give to children and other adults.

What is fascinating about infants and toddlers is their courage to take on countless challenges. In contrast to adults, toddlers are eager to learn and they love challenges. Sadly, the parents' and teachers' loss of courage to engage in wide-ranging risk-taking shadows children's learning adventuresomeness. Adults' fear of failure has led them to 'play it safe', not risk-take and go for the average. It is for the latter reason that the majority of schoolchildren attain only average results.

The doubts adults have about their own competency are manifested in the discouragement of children's efforts to do things for themselves and to take on new activities.

The opposite of discouragement is encouragement, and, next to the giving and receiving of love, it is the most important aspect of childrearing. The lack of encouragement is certainly one of the basic causes of children's difficult behaviours. Very often children who present with distressing behaviours are children whose spontaneity and eagerness to learn have been frequently discouraged. Parents have forgotten the old adage 'never do for a child what he can do for himself'. Here is an example of how a parent may unwittingly discourage a child:

> John, aged five, was in the garden watching his dad mow the lawn. Dad had stopped mowing and had begun to rake the cut grass. John eagerly asked his dad, 'Could I do that'? 'No John!' he said crossly. 'You're too small. Best that I do it. Wait until you are bigger.'

The excitement and adventure of that challenge have been considerably dampened down for John. In a thousand subtle ways – by word, by tone of voice, by facial expression and by action, we indicate to children that we consider them small, inept, unskilled and generally inferior. The wonder of it is that children persist in trying to become competent at all. Of course, while there are some children who at least go for an average level of competency, there are others who become apathetic around learning.

At the other extreme, there are children who are driven to learn from fear, and they tend to become perfectionists; they suffer from an over-encouragement, not to learn but to perform to a perfectionistic standard. They too have lost the adventure of learning.

Impatience with a child's efforts to do things for himself is another way of extinguishing a child's love of challenge, as shown in the following example:

Three-year-old Mark was determined to carry his own rucksack to the aeroplane with his parents. He was struggling and falling behind, but, nonetheless, there was a look of satisfaction on his face. His father says, 'Come here, Mark. Let me carry that for you. You are too slow.'

Mark is made to feel inefficient in the face of his father's ability to carry things easily. A further humiliation is that not only does his father take his rucksack from him, but he also picks him up and carries him. Not surprisingly, the child lets out cries of protest, but to no avail. He is now seen as 'difficult and ungrateful'.

Parental love is best shown through regular encouragement towards independence. This determination to enable children to do things for themselves needs to start at birth and be maintained all through childhood and adolesence. It is an attitude that needs to guide parents through all daily challenges and situations of childrearing. Children have immense courage and it is the responsibility of adults to help them to apply and maintain it.

The problem for some parents in encouraging children's independence is that they have lost their own courage, and their cautiousness blocks them from practising this essential aspect of parenting. It is important, therefore, for parents to recognise their own limitations, which are a product of their own childhood experiences.

There is no way that criticism and condemnation of parents who discourage children's efforts to do things for themselves are inferred. What those parents require is understanding, help and to be shown ways out of the present difficulties. There is no intention to heap further discouragement onto the heads of bewildered and discouraged parents. Nevertheless, the importance of parents re-discovering their own courage cannot be over-emphasised. Dwelling on mistakes and failures saps courage. Embrace the mistake, as it provides you with the wonderful opportunity to progress in becoming more competent. And when you try something new and it works, be sure to encourage your willingness to try new things. Remember, failure and success are integral to each other and can neither add nor detract from your personal value. This will do much to maintain your own courage. Remember, too, that it is the challenge that counts and the aim is only for improvement, not perfection. Notice and enjoy the little improvements and trust in your limitless ability to improve further.

## Q11. HAVE WE FORGOTTEN HOW BEING BELITTLED AS CHILDREN HAD A DEVASTATING EFFECT ON US? IT APPEARS WE HAVE, BECAUSE SOME OF US REPEAT THE BELITTLING. WHY?

Nearly thirty years ago the founder of the American Mental Health Association said: 'Everything you need to know about mental health can be summed up in only two words: don't belittle'. If everyone would practise this two-word prescription, if everyone would live by these two words: 'don't belittle', then 95 per cent of the mental health problems we deal with today could be eliminated.

To belittle is to put someone down, to make them feel small. It means to be judgemental and critical in ways that lessen another's sense of self.

There are innumerable ways of demeaning another's presence – superiority, discouragement, cynicism, sarcasm, irritability, dismissiveness, unkindness, not listening, advising, over-protection, impatience, non-celebration of key events in a person's life, comparison, competitiveness, dominance, distance, remoteness, lack of emotion. A lot of the problems we see today – crime, physical, sexual and emotional violations, broken homes, poor academic progress, addictions and conflict in the workplace – can be traced to belittling.

How often you experience belittling (several times a week or a day), how fierce or severe the 'put-down' is, and how long over time (one month, a year, two years, ten years, twenty years) you have endured such blows to self-worth, are what need to be considered.

The frequency, intensity and endurance over time of being bullied are important determinants of how low the self-esteem of the person can go. Belittling can occur in all relationships – in homes, classrooms, communities, workplaces, hospitals, sports clubs, churches and countries.

Leaders (parents, teachers, bosses, supervisors, priests, politicians, club leaders, doctors, nurses) play a crucial role in determining the ethos of the social system of which they are in charge. The leader who belittles can create a dark ethos, wherein belittling of each other becomes the norm.

The antidote to belittling is to lift people up, to respect differences, to cherish the uniqueness and giftedness of every person and to encourage them to value themselves. Most of all, it means to love and be loved, and to celebrate each person's individual expression of their uniqueness. The antidote entails listening, encouragement, understanding, compassion and positive discipline.

Whilst I agree with the two-word ethos 'don't belittle', there is something fundamental missing from this important principle for mental health. The missing link makes it unlikely that the prescription 'don't belittle' will have any significant influence, which may be one of the reasons I am writing about this issue thirty years later. What is missing is that those who belittle others do so to protect their own poor sense of self and from a fear of being demeaned.

There is something truly revealing about the low self-esteem of those who knock others. When you break the words up into 'don't be little', you see that the prescription has to be applied to the self before you can be in a place to lift up the self of another.

There is a wonderful line in a poem by Marianne Williamson: 'Your playing small does not serve the world.' Indeed, when I play little or small, and when I belittle or make another feel small, I hurt both myself and the other person. I am subconsciously revealing my own low sense of self; the belittling of another is a projection of my experience of being demeaned, which is now being mirrored back to liberate me from my fears. I may need support from friends, or from a counselling psychologist to help me free myself from my defensive behaviour. If not, I continue to cast shadows on the presence of those with whom I defensively interact. Only when I recognise and take action against my belittling of others will I see that I must value myself before I can be ready to affirm and lift up others.

## Q12. ISN'T IT TRUE THAT A GOOD SPANKING NEVER DOES A CHILD ANY HARM?

There was a time when punishment of children was the primary means of educating them on what was right and wrong behaviour. Parents, teachers and other adults believed they had a right to dominate and have power over children. What is often forgotten is that most adults were dominated by people in authority – priests, doctors, teachers and bosses. We lived in an autocratic social system in which those in authority reserved the privilege to themselves of meting out rewards or punishment according to merits. The Catholic Church and educational system were masters in the exercising of this autocratic code of living. It is not surprising that such dominant means of influencing others was imitated by parents towards children.

Even though we have moved towards a great realisation of democracy as a way of life, many of the old punishment strategies persist in the parenting and educating of children. However, since democracy implies equality, parents and teachers can no longer assume the role of the 'authority'. Traditionally, authority equalled dominance, but its true meaning is 'authorship of self'. In a democracy, one individual cannot be allowed to have control over another, whether parent-child, teacher-student, child-child, boss-employee, husband-wife, priest-believer. Dominance, force and overpowering need to be substituted with equality, cooperation and respect.

Whether adults accept it or not, children know they have gained an equal social status with adults and that adults no longer enjoy a superior position to them. Adult power over them is gone and children 'know' it.

Adults need to realise the futility of attempting to impose their will upon children. Rarely does any amount of physical hurting (now illegal) or emotional hurting of children bring about lasting submission. When it does, adults doom children to a life of passivity, fear, timidity and powerlessness or one of counter-dominance, aggression and rebelliousness. Thankfully, many of today's children are willing to take any amount of physical or emotional punishment in order to assert their 'rights'. Confused and bewildered parents and teachers who have not been trained in democratic ways of rearing and teaching children, hope that punishment will eventually bring about results, and blind themselves to the fact that they are actually getting nowhere with their autocratic methods. At best, temporary obedience may be gained, but the losses far outweigh the gains – lowering of children's self-esteem, estranged relationship between adult and child, guilt feelings on the part of the adult who meted out the punishment and missed opportunity to help the child learn self-control.

Understanding the intention behind a child's difficult behaviour is an essential parental skill. The following example illustrates the benefits of this skill:

> In spite of being spanked, humiliated, deprived of privileges, seven-year-old Mark continued to soil and to wet his bed. His mother and father could not understand why the child persisted with these 'wrongdoings' – they were at the end of their tether. 'Oh, Mark! What are we going to do with you?' Both parents had very successful professional careers and employed a full-time childminder for Mark. They both arrived home late in the evenings and needed to leave early in the mornings to get to their respective places of work.

Mark's mother complained to me 'We just don't have the time to be dealing with these problems – what can you do about it?' It seemed to me that the child's soiling and bed-wetting was saying 'I feel you don't give a shit about me', 'I'm totally pissed off' and 'At least you know I'm around when I'm bad'. Understanding the hidden intention of children's (and, indeed, adults') troubled behaviours is essential to finding a lasting solution. I encouraged the parents to find quality time to be with their child so that he did not have to use 'attention-seeking' ways to get them to love him. It is also important to see that there is wisdom in the child punishing his parents with his difficult behaviours, in that he hopes they may feel the punishing effects of the loss of love he is experiencing.

When it comes to a 'battle' between parents and children, children are far more resilient and tenacious than adults. They can out-plot, out-manoeuvre and out-last their parents and teachers. Many adults who have charge of children come to the end of their endurance, shake their heads and cry out in desperation 'I don't know what to do anymore!' What these adults often forget is that children learn their punishing methods from adults.

Children need adult leadership. An effective leader inspires and stimulates others into actions that suit the situation. So it needs to be with parents. Children need adult guidance. They will accept this guidance when they see that they are accepted as equal human beings with equal rights to decide what they will do. Parents and teachers can learn to employ more effective and democratic methods to stimulate children so that they have a desire to cooperate with the demands of particular situations. Adults can create an atmosphere of mutual self-respect and consideration and provide opportunities for children to live happily and cooperatively with others. Respect for self and the child is central to meeting requests of children. And all of this can be done without overpowering, for overpowering incites rebellion and is counter-productive to the aim of child-rearing – respect for self and others and self-control.

## Q13.  HOW CAN I IDENTIFY WHEN MY CHILD IS TROUBLED?

It is not difficult for adults to identify the child who is troubled. What is difficult, particularly for the parents (and sometimes teachers), is to admit to the fact that their child may be undergoing a crisis. I have known of parents who, out of a subconscious defensiveness, have rationalised that 'it's a passing phase' or 'it's due to his diet' or some other vague biological explanation. When parents are in a place of denial or rationalisation, it is they who need help first. Indeed, the very fact that the parents feel emotionally threatened by their child's troubled symptoms indicates that the possible cause of the child's distress lies within the family. Of course, not all troubled behaviour of children can be traced to family dynamics. Children can be equally under emotional, physical, social and sexual threat within the other social systems they frequent – school, community and sports clubs.

Signs of children's hidden conflicts can be usefully grouped under these headings:

- Physical signs
- Under-control signs
- Over-control signs

Examples of possible physical manifestations of distress are: nail-biting, bed-wetting, soiling, headaches, abdominal pain, jumping at sudden noises, involuntary muscle spasms, obesity or skin problems.

Signs of under-control include those behaviours that may be very troublesome and annoying to others but are, none-theless, clear signs of emotional distress. Children displaying these signs are acting out their inner turmoil in a sub-conscious attempt to get their unmet needs recognised and met. Typical under-control manifestations of distress are: rebellious behaviour, verbal aggressiveness, destructiveness of property, hyperactivity and bullying. Psychologically, these difficult behaviours are saying something right about the child, but socially, the behaviours can make it difficult for parents and others. The danger is that parents can respond defensively to these manifestations, thereby adding fuel to the fire, with the resultant escalation of the child's under-control behaviours. The 'out-of-control' punishing response by parents serves only to convince the child of his inadequacy and unlovability, and plunges him into further depths of insecurity.

Because children's under-control behaviours can be so upsetting to other family members, some constructive action is of course needed to try to reduce or eliminate them. However, such a course of action will have little hope of being effective if it is not coupled with attempts to understand what is emotionally troubling the child.

Girls are more likely than boys to exhibit over-control signs of distress. Examples include shyness, passivity, perfectionism, timidity, over-pleasing, feeling easily hurt. These manifestations do not in any serious way disrupt the lives of others. Quiet, shy children do not interfere with parents in carrying out their domestic and other responsibilities. It is for this reason that children showing under-control signs of distress are more often sent to clinical psychologists or counsellors for help. Unfortunately, the children who are perfectionistic, timid and fearful are more at risk emotionally than those children who 'act out' their feelings of rejection and inadequacy. It is as if those who shout loudest are more likely to be heard.

The hope is that children, whether they exhibit under-control or over-control signs of distress, will have their emotional conflicts detected and effectively responded to, and the more adaptive ways of expressing their fears, worries and insecurities will be modelled and taught to them.

The first step is to *listen*. Listening is an act of worship and when parents genuinely demonstrate that they want to actively listen, children may open up and reveal their inner worries. The second step is to *understand*. The word 'understand', when it is broken down to under-stand, sets the course of action required. The child's *stand* may be aggression (under-control) or timidity (over-control), and what the parent needs to do is get under, go beneath the behavioural signs and discover what is causing the child's distress.

*Patience* is essential, as it provides the safety for children to reveal why they are behaving in troubled ways. Any attempt on the part of the parent to force their way into the hidden world of children will only result in the child heightening and expanding his protectors.

The fourth requirement is *compassion*. Compassion provides the unconditional love and intuitive wisdom that *knows* that children are not deliberately trying to make their parents' lives difficult but are attempting to bring to the fore what they have not dared to reveal up to this point of time.

I can guarantee parents that when they actively listen, understand, be patient and show compassion, their children will open up and will in turn show the same wise responses to them.

## Q14. IF CHILDREN LEARN SO MUCH THROUGH OBSERVATION, IS THERE ANY NEED TO SPEND TIME ON TRAINING THEM TO ACQUIRE CERTAIN SKILLS?

One of the many responsibilities of parents is training their children for the many challenges of living. While children learn many skills through observation, parents cannot afford to rely on children learning everything this way. In any case, the quality of modelling living skills may not always be the best. Indeed, when the latter is the case it would be wise for parents to improve their own living skills before launching into the training of children.

Children require training in how to be hygienic, how to dress, how to tie their shoes, how to eat, how to safely cross the street and, gradually, they can be introduced to taking on tasks around the home. None of these skills can be learned by incidental remarks, nor through impatience, cajoling, scolding or threat of punishment. When learning any behaviour that is likely to become a source of threat to self, children cleverly create all sorts of ways not to attend to what is being asked of them. Worse still, they may become the 'goodie-good' children eager to please and terrified of displeasing. Time for training needs to be part and parcel of the daily routine and it is imperative that such training is done in an adventurous, fun and loving way.

When parents do not take the time to train children, they will later spend a great deal more time correcting the child who has not been given the structured opportunities to learn life skills. When parents resort to constant corrections rather than systematic training, children will not learn because they perceive the correction as criticism and a lack of belief in their 'response-ableness'. Consequently, they may become discouraged and rebellious. Furthermore, the constant corrections can be cleverly employed by children as a means of getting special attention, and children like to provoke repetition as it gives them a feeling of power over adults.

Children who are encouraged love to learn and seek out challenges. Parents who are alert to their child's eagerness to learn recognise such efforts and encourage them. However, it is advisable that definite periods be set aside for more effective learning to take place. 'Critical times' in a household, such as the morning rush hour, mealtimes, bedtimes or when parents are tired after a day's work, are scarcely the times for training. The presence and strain of these 'critical' times may trigger impatience and annoyance in the parent and rebellion in the children. When both parents are working, some of this training may need to be done by the childminder.

Afternoon playtime is an opportune time for training in a new skill or enhancing a skill that is emerging. Countless training aids can be got on the toy market. Or the trainer can create his or her own teaching tools – using old shirts and used shoes for training in tying buttons and tying laces. Table manners can be taught with doll tea parties. At the same time, introductions and the way to welcome guests can become part of the party. Training for responsible behaviour on the bus or train and in the car can be done with pretend rides. Similarly, visits to the supermarket can be staged by the children creating their own shop, and this is another way of introducing them to the reality that supermarkets are for shopping, not for playing. Appropriate behaviour in other people's homes and in restaurants can be similarly developed. Acting and role-playing are ideal training aids, since children are born actors.

Training in any skill needs to be taken up in a repeated daily routine until the particular skill is learned. Each skill is best taught separately. Patience, fun, a belief in the child's limitless ability to learn and encouragement are fundamental to creating the positive atmosphere that is required for children to learn life skills.

## Q15. MY CHILD IS ADAMANT THAT 'I CAN DO IT MYSELF', BUT I FEEL HE SHOULD ACCEPT MY HELP. WHAT DO YOU SUGGEST?

Toddlers and young children have a strong innate drive to be independent and self-sufficient. Most parents have encountered their child digging in his heels and protesting 'I want to do it myself'. Parents do children no favours when they do something for a child that he can do or learn to do for himself. A rule of thumb that adults who have responsibility for children need to follow is: 'Never do for a child what he can do for himself.'

Some parents react to this childrearing rule by protesting: 'But I want to do everything for my child. I just love taking care of him. He's everything I've got.' Another common response is 'She won't be a child for long.'

If such parents realised what they are doing to their child they would be horrified. Some personal insecurity or loss from their childhood years is blinding them to the wisdom of fostering independence in children from their earliest years. 'My child will have all the things and opportunities that I was never given as a child' is not an uncommon source of over-involved parenting.

When a parent does everything for a child, unwittingly the child is being taught that he is dependent, helpless, inferior, inadequate and useless. Cleverly, the child will perceive that to show power and independence would be dangerous and would result in rejection by the over-protective parent. Ironically, by recognising the parent's vulnerability and the expediency of conforming to his parent's ways, the child manifests his genius. However, the problem is that the child's capability is being channelled into defensive strategies that protect him from hurt and rejection, with the result that mature progress towards independence is now solidly blocked.

Whenever adults do something for a child which he can do for himself, there is some subconscious craving in those adults to be needed. In order to have that need met, the parent has to appear bigger than the child, better, more capable, more deft, more experienced and more important. Quite subconsciously, the parent only feels secure when the child totally depends on her.

Doing for a child what he can do for himself takes the heart out of children's love of learning, natural curiosity and eagerness to learn. Such seemingly benign parenting deprives children of the opportunities to explore their vast potential and unique giftedness. Over-protective parents rob children of their security, which is based on the realisation of their own expansive capacity to do things for themselves and problem-solve when challenges are encountered. Not only that, children are blocked from exercising their right to stand on their own two feet, to be independent and self-sufficient.

There is no doubt that there are times when a child will try to slide out of responsibility and be quite happy for a parent to take over for him. In such a situation the wise parent keeps to her determination to encourage the child to do things for himself. It is crucial that the parent remains patient, because impatience, irritability or comparison with an older (or younger) child exhibiting more competence can quickly dry up the wellspring of enthusiasm to learn within children.

The littleness of children is very appealing and our first impulse is to reach out and help a child when he is having a little struggle with what he is attempting to do. For example, the infant reaches for the spoon because he wants to feed himself. All too frequently, parents block these early attempts in order to avoid the mess, thereby discouraging these first steps towards independence. What a tragedy! It is much easier to clean up the mess than to revitalise the child's lost drive to do things for himself.

As soon as children show initiative, parents need to take full advantage of it and let them experiment as much as possible. You'd be surprised how quickly children learn when they are encouraged and positively supported. There are countless opportunities for children to experience their capability. At times children require help, supervision, encouragement and training, which their parents need to supply. Provision of these aids to learning means helping the child to do things for himself and not doing it for him.

No parent wants to consciously block a child's independence, but a parent's emotional baggage can have that effect. When a parent or another adult observes that a child is not being stimulated to achieve independence, then caring confrontation is required. It is a truism that parents can only bring children to the same level of independence they have reached themselves, and their over-protection of children is always a mirror of their own dependence.

## Q16. SHOULD CHILDREN BE PAID TO DO CHORES?

The system of rewarding children for good behaviour is as blocking of their maturity as the system of punishment. A similar lack of respect is demonstrated when adults reward each other for favours or for good deeds. In a home, school or workplace of mutual respect among equals, a job is done because it needs doing, and the satisfaction comes from the harmony of two or more people doing a job together.

In the scene described below the child has no concept of how he has done his bit towards contributing to the family welfare. His attention is centred on 'what's in it for me'.

Michael, aged ten, was given €5 to get some messages for his father in the local shop. When he returned, his father thanked him and asked him for the change. 'Why do you want the change?' Michael sulkily asked. 'Why, Michael, because I need it.' Angrily, the boy deposited the change on the table. 'I did you a favour, didn't I?' he said under his breath. Puzzled, his father looked at him. 'Yes, you did a *favour*!'

It is not good practice that children be paid to do chores. They live in the house, are provided with many comforts, eat the food, are clothed and share in many other benefits. If they are the equals they now claim to be, they are obliged to share the toil.

When children are tangibly rewarded for chores, they assume that they need not do anything unless there is something in it for them. No opportunities to develop a sense of responsibility are provided under these circumstances. The emphasis has been placed on 'what's in it for me.'

Children need to be part of the whole scene of family life. Such responsibility needs to start as early as possible, at the point when a child can do things for himself and others. Responsibilities need to increase with age. Children also need to have a share in the family's spending money, usually in the form of an allowance, which needs to increase as the child gets older. It is not wise to have any connection at all between chores and allowances. Children are requested to do chores because they contribute to the family welfare. They are given allowances because they share the benefits, and they need to be allowed to spend their allowance in any way they like.

In the same way that it is not advisable for parents to reward children for doing chores, neither is it wise to reward children for their cooperation. The following typical family scene brings home this point:

Mother and father were going out for the evening and leaving their two small children with a babysitter. As soon as they began to go out of the house, the children started to cry. 'Be good now and we'll bring you back a toy each'. 'What kind?' the two children asked. 'Oh I don't know – something', their mother answered hastily as she got out the front door.

Both parents are attempting to gain cooperation by promising material gains. Children do not need 'bribes' to be good. They actually want to be good. Good behaviour on the part of children springs from their drive to belong to the family and to the home, to contribute usefully and to cooperate. When parents, teachers and other adults bribe a child for good behaviour, they are in effect showing him that they do not trust him, which is a form of discouragement.

Parents face a serious challenge if their children refuse to cooperate without an answer to the question, 'What's in it for me?' Unless the child views the reward as adequate, why would he bother to cooperate? An attitude of materialism is now developed, since such children assume that the world owes them everything. If nothing is automatically forthcoming he or she will 'show them'.

The end result of using material rewards to gain children's cooperation is the development of an attitude that says 'if they have not rewarded me, I shall punish them with difficult behaviour – sulk, rage, disrupt'. It is vital to understand that the child is responding to how his parents typically relate to him – he is conforming to their materialistic ways. Furthermore, he does not feel seen and trusted for himself, but only for what he does. Demanding the reward gains him some recognition.

Satisfaction comes from a sense of contribution and participation – a sense frequently denied to those children who are daily exposed to the parental (or classroom) system of rewarding them with material things. In our misguided efforts to gain cooperation through rewards, we effectively deny children the basic satisfaction of living. Certainly, show verbal appreciation of children's specific efforts to participate in family and classroom life, but it is best that tangible rewards are not tied to their responsibilites, but rather given spontaneously with no strings attached.

## Q17. IS IT IMPORTANT THAT CHILDREN EXPERIENCE ALONENESS?

Aloneness is the foundation for inner security and of all creativity, since it is only in such a state that it is possible to explore one's internal world. The word 'aloneness' when hyphenated shows its true meaning: 'al-one-ness'. One-ness with one's unique, sacred, capable and creative self is the solid ground from which no one can exile, exclude or in any way diminish you.

There are many adults who find it extremely difficult to be alone, who cannot embrace time for self and who depend on relationships for any sense of security. If these adults do not have a stable, ongoing relationship with another, they suffer chronic feelings of aloneness and loneliness. Paradoxically, when you are comfortable with your own company and enjoy exploring your own interiority, you rarely encounter loneliness. Individuals who live from the inside out are like flowers to honeybees and draw many people to them. They also tend to maintain lifetime relationships because they manifest non-possessive closeness, openness, celebration of difference, safety, separateness and unobtrusiveness.

When you have not been given opportunities early on in childhood to embrace your aloneness, the innate need to be in possession of one's own person becomes projected onto others so that possession of another or being possessed by another becomes the substitute goal. This substitute goal reflects accurately your need to join with yourself and move towards being not only the guardian of your own solitude, but that of your partner or friend as well.

Parents, childminders and teachers equally have a responsibility to embrace their own aloneness, so that they are in a position to provide the opportunities for each child to develop his or her own positive sense of aloneness. For the child to accomplish this fundamental life task, the significant adults in his life need to create an environment in which it is safe to be nobody (not having to prove himself), because it is only out of such a place that the child can begin to discover himself. Once the child feels he has to be a certain way in his parents' eyes, the child has to remain on guard, mobilised to respond to his parents' projections. It is not safe for the child to float away into his own inner experience. For example, parents who are constantly anxious about a child's welfare do not provide the safety and space for the child to go into his inner world. The child cleverly learns to be alert to his parents' anxiety and so lives life from the outside in.

A parent needs to be in touch with her own positive aloneness in order to *hold* a child, not just physically, but in silence. In fostering a state of separateness by being present, but not interfering, a parent creates a *holding* environment that nourishes a child. In so doing, this parent sustains and encourages her child's inner life. Similarly, not doing things that a child can do for himself maintains this safe environment for the development of the child's sense of an inner and vastly capable self.

It is important to see that the capacity to be alone is a paradox, since it can only be developed with someone else in the room. For that reason, a child who is left *too alone* struggles with being at home with herself just as much as the child who is too *intruded upon.*

Comfort with one's aloneness can only develop when the *holding* environment is safe and non-intrusive. Once the capacity to be alone is developed, the child trusts that she will not be intruded upon and allows herself a secret communication with her private and personal experiences.

The best example I can think of for the process of developing children's capacity to be alone is that silent holding between two adults, who sense their deep love for each other, and yet each is content to be alone, but not withdrawn. No anxiety exists; indeed each feels safe in the security of being loved for self and there is no doubt about the other partner's availability, but there is also no need for active contact. It is in this way we can also develop an unintrusive holding of children.

## Q18.  CHILDREN DESERVE TO BE GIVEN TOYS, DON'T THEY?

Buying children toys was once a seasonal task, but many parents succumb to random buying of toys for children. Parents engage in frequent toy buying for many reasons – inability to say 'no', wanting to be liked, 'for peace sake', 'to keep up with the Jones's – but there is a danger that the child will conclude that 'if Mum doesn't buy me a toy, she doesn't love me anymore'. In such a situation the toy holds little value, but getting the parent to give becomes all-important.

There is absolutely no reason why a parent should purchase a child every toy the child sees and wants. Nor is there any sound sense to getting her something every time she accompanies you when your are shopping. Such indiscriminate buying pampers a child's whims and makes her feel that these purchases are her right.

It is best that toys have a useful purpose or meet a given need. Furthermore, toy presents are best given on special days when presents are expected and are a token of our recognition of the specialness of the child in our lives. Seasonal purchasing of meaningful toys also makes sense – indoor games for the winter, outdoor games for the spring and summer and so on. It is essential that shopping is purposeful. Children learn from you and they form their ideas about money and about shopping when they go with you. When there is no limit to what they can demand, they assume that the supply of money is endless and their sense of the value of material things becomes distorted.

Many parents are well aware of the discarded toys and puppies that were the consequence of non-purposeful or over-indulgence of children, not just from parents but also from well-meaning but misguided relatives. I am not suggesting that we do not give presents – and this applies equally to giving presents to adults – but I am suggesting that presents be bought with thought to their usefulness and value. 'It is the thought that counts': that is what gives meaning to present-giving, not the size or monetary value of the present.

Another issue that deserves consideration around present-giving is the brand name. There are adolescents who will hound their parents to get the 'in' designer brand because they would be hugely embarrassed to face their peers with an unknown brand, say, of runners. Is it wise to give in to these demands, even though some parents are put to the pin of their collar to purchase the more expensive designer labels? Do we need to understand that the young person may be ridiculed by his peers when he wears an unrecognisable brand of runners? Certainly, it is important to listen to young people and their fears of how their peers see and react to them. However, when we support them in their fears concerning their peers, we are doing them no favours as we are colluding with their dependence on others. The most common addiction among adults is the addiction to what other people think. This dependence cripples autonomy and the development of independence. Parents and other adults need to guide children into living their own lives, to live from the inside out and not from the outside in. However, when parents themselves are controlled by what others think of them, they are unlikely to encourage their child to assert his own unique identity and individuality and not hide his uniqueness behind a designer name or in approval-seeking from his peer group. There is nothing more unique than the individual presence of each person; no brand name adds to that. If you believe a designer label adds to your presence, you have an addiction. Such enmeshment of a person's identity with a commercial brand name is heavily and lucratively exploited by fashion designers and toy and sportswear manufacturers.

A final issue regarding gift-giving is that it is a two-way street, in that the giving of a gift is as pleasurable as the receiving of one. It is important that children are encouraged to be sensitive and responsive to the needs of others for acknowledgement, particularly parents. The give and take is what makes for mature relationships.

## Q19. HOW CAN I BEST DISCIPLINE CHILDREN'S DIFFICULT BEHAVIOUR?

The need for discipline arises when certain behaviours threaten the welfare and rights of others. Generally speaking, aggressive or 'out-of-control' type behaviours are the targets for disciplinary practices. However, what is often not appreciated is that 'over-controlled' behaviours such as passivity are also a source of neglect and need to come under the umbrella of 'ill-disciplined' behaviour. Turning a blind eye and passivity have resulted in the neglect of the welfare of many children and adults in this country. However, I feel we are a long way off from applying sanctions to passive-type behaviours in homes, schools, communities and workplaces. Nevertheless, the 'demonisation' of aggressive behaviours needs to be balanced with the 'de-sanctification' of passivity.

The empowerment of those who are passive (afraid of showing power) is just as important as the empowerment of those who are aggressive and disruptive (which are attempts to overpower). When individuals are self-possessed and in touch with their 'power beyond measure' (in the words of Nelson Mandela), there is no need to resort to the defensive behaviours of aggression or passivity. That is why in social systems where there are discipline difficulties, an anti-passivity campaign is just as expedient as an anti-bullying one. Action on discipline problems is the responsibility not only of each individual member of a social system, but also of the system itself. There still are homes, schools, work-places, communities and sporting organisations that do not have strong back-up systems to deal with neglect that is of an aggressive or passive nature.

One of the myriad challenges that faces us is the acknowl-edgement that most discipline practices are actually abusive in nature, thereby leading to an escalation of problems rather than the desired effect of problem reduction. A further challenge is to develop true discipline procedures that do not violate the rights of those who perpetrate ill-disciplined conduct. Two wrongs do not make a right. In any case, it makes no sense to fight fire with fire and an attempt to overpower only reinforces the overpowering aspect of undisciplined behaviour.

The discipline of old, which is still largely practised, was ill-conceived. It was based on the false notion that children (and adults) are fundamentally bad and that the bad should be beaten out of them (by word or deed) and good beaten into them. What is central to any effective discipline approach is the sacredness of each human being and the belief in the fundamental goodness of each person. Certainly, difficult behaviours need to be dealt with, but in a way that does not demean a person's presence or threaten the rights of the person to physical, sexual, intellectual, emotional, social, creative and spiritual safety.

There are still those who believe that parents have a right to physically chastise children. Violence breeds violence and parents who physically slap children are actually giving children permission to use physical force to get their own way in life. It is, therefore, not surprising that one in five women are still subjected to violence and violence between men still hits the daily headlines. Bullying in the workplace is still commonplace.

When adults, in disciplining difficult behaviours, physically slap, push, shove and pull a person, that person's physical rights are violated. When discipline involves labelling a person 'a fool' or 'a thickhead', that person's intellectual rights are violated. When feelings are ridiculed or laughed at or a person is labelled 'cry-baby', 'Mammy's little boy', 'weakling', that person's emotional rights are violated. When a person is publicly humiliated, his social rights are violated. It carries no weight to say that those who have acted aggressively have violated the rights of others (which indeed they have) and that they deserve the same treatment in return. This is the case of the pot calling the kettle black. All such responses are not disciplinary responses.

True discipline is not about control or punishment; rather it involves the vindication and safeguarding of people's rights and the restoration of violated rights. This responsibility lies with those who have been at the receiving end of ill-disciplined behaviour in the social system of which they are a member. Those who have perpetrated the undesirable actions are often not in a place to be responsible, and for that reason the old discipline of emphasis on the perpetrator was not effective.

The use of sanctions is to provide sanctuary to those whose rights have been violated. The whole aim of discipline needs to focus on those who have been victimised and the steps needed to restore safety and protection for their rights.

Certainly, those who have lost control, particularly those who persistently offend, need help to discover and resolve the reasons why they have acted in such a way. However, this is beyond a discipline issue and must not dilute in any way the actions needed to restore violated rights to those who have been victimised.

## Q20. WHAT IS THE BEST WAY OF DEALING WITH BULLYING?

It comes as no surprise that Irish schools face a raft of legal suits for failing to take action against playground bullying. Frustrated that schools were not doing enough to protect their children, a considerable number of parents have initiated legal proceedings. Other legal actions are being taken by adults who were harassed as children and, in spite of reporting to the teachers that they were being bullied, no action was taken on their behalf.

Children need to have the security that significant adults in their lives – parents and teachers – will champion them when they are bullied either by peers or by adults. All children deserve safety in all of the social systems they frequent – home, school, community, church and sports clubs. Certainly, there is now a greater awareness in Irish society of the importance of both physical and sexual safety for children. However, as a society we are still a long way from accepting that the *emotional* threats to children are far more prevalent. Indeed, it is a truism that people – adults and children alike – regularly emotionally hurt each other. Emotional hurting has many faces, for example, criticism, ridicule, scolding, hostile humour, put-down messages, comparisons, cynicism, sarcasm, dismissiveness, impatience, intolerance, irritability and aggression.

One of the most frequent emotional neglects is passivity, where individuals turn a blind eye to children or adults being demeaned, lessened, exiled, humiliated and ignored. Clearly, the frequency, intensity and duration in the immediate threatening situation and over time of passive (and aggressive) actions are serious factors to consider. One wonders what those children who are at the mercy of bullying behaviours from other children or adults think of those adults who are aware of the sad circumstances but do nothing? And what about those young people who go around harassing their peers or adults and are not challenged by adults? It needs to be seen that being passive in the face of bullying is as serious a neglect of children as the bullying itself. For too long Irish society has demonised those who exhibit aggression but sanctified those who are passive. Passivity in an adult masks a great neglect of self and of others, particularly children. Aggression, too, masks a great neglect of self and, more obviously, of others. Both defensive behaviours need to be challenged, not in a way that judges but in a way that understands. Understanding what makes an individual aggressive or passive is fundamental to bringing about responsible behaviour. Judgement, ridicule and condemnation, whether of bullying or passivity, are equally defensive responses and are unlikely to bring about the desired changes.

Understanding means getting to the core of what lies under the aggressive or passive stand of an adult or child and attempting to bring forward what lies hidden. Typically, deep hurt lies at the heart of aggression and passivity. The intention of both aggression and passivity is to prevent further hurt or at least to minimise its occurrence. Helping those individuals to break the silence on their hurts and the source of their hurts is essential. What is also crucial is providing the support for the child or adult who employs passivity or aggression to express strongly, but respectfully, their rights to physical, sexual, emotional, intellectual, social and spiritual safety no matter where they are or whom they encounter.

Understanding threatening behaviours does not mean excusing them; on the contrary, the defensive behaviours of an adult or child cannot be allowed to become a threat to others. Sanctions and the provision of opportunities for the emergence of mature behaviour need to be the consequences of threatening behaviours. Prevention of such threats lies in the hands of all of us by ensuring the establishment of safety for members, young and old, of each social system.

## Q21. HOW IS TELEVISION VIEWING BEST MANAGED IN A FAMILY?

In almost every home the television set creates many conflicts. There are heated exchanges about what to watch or who will watch what. Parents are concerned about wrong impressions the children receive. They worry too about such passive entertainment with so much time spent on watching 'trash'. School homework is neglected when children watch the 'really good' evening programmes. Bedtime becomes a difficult challenge because the 'best' programmes come on late. Mealtime is regulated by television programmes. Many families have even changed their dining times and now eat in front of the television or have an extra television in the kitchen/dining room; each member is isolated in his or her absorption in the programme. Some parents fret that mealtimes are no longer a social opportunity for the promotion of family harmony. Mothers who put considerable energy and creativity into meal preparation and presentation feel that their efforts are not appreciated; indeed, some mothers feel like putting their fist through the television screen. Instead, these mothers attempt to control the situation by removing the television from the dining area and insisting nobody leaves the table during mealtimes to go and watch television. Quarrels and dissension ensue. Some parents even refuse to have a television in the house, with the result that the children either go to the neighbour to watch or keep up running complaints about how unfair their parents are, particularly when all the other children are allowed to watch television.

Whether parents like it or not, television is here to stay. It presents challenges that we need to take on rather than resent.

When children fight over who gets to see what programme, parents may either let them solve it themselves or turn off the television until an agreement is reached. When the quarrel involves both the parents and the children, the situation poses extra difficulties. Many parents believe that it is their right to watch the evening programmes, and, whether they like it or not, the children have to accept this situation. However, this is not a wise practice as it is coercive rather than discursive.

Television viewing is a family issue and any differences that arise are best solved by the family all together. Such an approach eliminates double standards and promotes equality among all members of the family. The challenge is to ask 'what are we as a family going to do about disputes about television viewing?', rather than the parents saying 'what do I need to do to solve the problem?' All members of the family need to come to an agreement together. If the dissension is very fraught, the parent can remove the fuse for the television set(s), and no one, including the parents, watches any programmes until an agreement is reached.

Mealtimes and the importance of 'family time', as well as respect for the person who prepares the meals and appreciation for the daily efforts made in meal preparation,  are also important issues for the family to consider. Some flexibility is always needed around any decision reached so that, for example, when the family decides on 'no television at mealtimes', an important event on television (Ireland playing Iran, for instance!) may occasionally take precedence.

Establishing a time for school homework and a time for television viewing is also an important family challenge and is best dealt with by parents reaching an understanding with children through discussion. The child may choose for himself what time he will watch television. His parents may then remain firm and hold him to his agreements by action, not words. Or if he is older, the question becomes 'what is to be done now?' Allow the adolescent to offer a solution.

If children want to watch television after their bedtime, parents need to be firm and consistent in order to maintain family routine. If the child is young, he is taken to bed without any negotiation. There is no power struggle involved if the parent does not have a personal stake in 'making him behave'. If the parent is firm in maintaining order and follows the demands of the situation, she or he merely takes him to bed. If the child is older, parents need to come to an agreement with him and then follow through on what he has agreed.

All of the above is not easy where parents have not managed to develop a relationship of trust and cooperation with their children. Actually, the television is not a problem in itself; it merely highlights the communication difficulties between parents and children.

The quality and content of the television programmes is not only a subject of parental concern, but also of national concern. Again, family discussion is the mature way to determine which programmes are desirable or non-desirable.

Parental concern for too much passive entertainment can be offset if parents make sure that there are other forms of interest and entertainment for individuals and for the family. Offering children pursuits of greater interest to stimulate and influence them often leads to children leaving the less desirable options.

# CHAPTER FOUR

# HOW CAN PARENTS BEST RESPOND TO CHILDREN'S CHALLENGING BEHAVIOURS?

- ☐ INTRODUCTION
- ☐ SPECIFIC QUESTIONS
  - Q1. I find I lose my temper when my child keeps engaging in an annoying behaviour, even though I have requested several times that she stop doing it. I feel guilty afterwards. Please help.
  - Q2. My child has certain bad habits which drive me wild. Nothing seems to work to get rid of them. Any ideas?
  - Q3. How do I manage a child/adolescent who is out of control?
  - Q4. My child is such a perfectionist. Is this a problem?
  - Q5. My child shows considerable aggression. How can I deal with it?
  - Q6. What is the best way to deal with a child's temper tantrums?
  - Q7. What can I do when my child creates an embarrassing scene in the supermarket?
  - Q8. How can I get the children to tidy up after themselves?
  - Q9. If my child is refusing to eat, what should I do?
  - Q10. I've tried everything to get my child to stop nail-biting, but without success. Any solutions?
  - Q11. Isn't a child who is constantly seeking attention just a plain nuisance?

Q12. I'm cracking up with my child's constant whining 'I want, I want, I want'. Is there anything I can do to stop this whining?

Q13. I feel helpless when my child cries. Can you help?

Q14. No matter what I say or do my oldest child keeps doing 'bad' things. Is there a reason for this?

Q15. My child reacts badly to being teased: any ideas why?

Q16. Why does my child constantly lie?

Q17. My children are constantly fighting with each other and it's driving me crazy! What can I do?

## INTRODUCTION

It is when children present with difficult behaviours that parents are more likely to reach out for answers. However, there are those parents who, because of their own unresolved deep vulnerability, do not seek help when children manifest challenging behaviours. There are those parents, too, who are in denial and thereby miss their children's cries for help. And there are parents who look for psychiatric labels for their children's challenging responses, and accept their children being put on psychotropic medication. It is not that these parents do not want the best for their children but, somehow, their children's challenging behaviours threaten their defensive 'comfort zone', and this threat is reduced by seeing the problem as being in the child. Teachers, too, resort to wanting children to be 'assessed', and presently there is an epidemic of children being labelled with the syndrome of ADDH (attention deficit disorder with hyperactivity) or ODD (oppositional defiance disorder), and Ritalin and Prozac are prescribed as solutions. These drugs may reduce the stress on the adults who have charge of these children, but they do little for the child.

It is also the case that parents are most likely to seek help for those behaviours in their children that most upset their lives, such as aggressive non-cooperation, temper tantrums, refusal to learn, eating problems, disruptiveness, hyperactivity, dyspraxia (clumsiness), learning difficulties, bullying, bed-wetting, soiling and whining. Parents are slower to spot that sometimes children need help when they are conformist and 'goodie-good' children who do not rock the boat. Often these latter children have clearly adapted to the unconscious, but nonetheless powerful, message: 'For peace sake don't upset your father' or 'For peace sake don't upset your mother'. In my own clinic, children are rarely referred by parents, or indeed, teachers, for such troubled behaviours as perfectionism, fearfulness, passivity, shyness, timidity, elective mutism and people-pleasing. The reason is that such passive-type responses do not upset adults' lives or challenge them to look to their own ways of relating to self and children. Nevertheless, both passive and aggressive behaviours are symptoms that need definite and caring responding. When conflict issues are not resolved in the family they continue to escalate and the next crisis will be worse than the previous one. The evidence for this is that children who manifest early indications of distress to which no heed was paid will manifest far greater distress symptoms later on. It is for this reason that in late adolescence and in young adulthood, more serious symptoms begin to appear. These symptoms, such as dropping out of school, depression, hallucinations, illusions, delusions, paranoia, obsessive-compulsiveness, extreme 'character' traits, anorexia nervosa, bulimia and alcohol or drug addiction, are not arising from genetic or hereditary defects, but from the unresolved conflicts within the family. It is a fact that when parents are not yet in a place of maturity to look closely at their adolescent's or young adult's manifested vulnerabilities, they are likely to feel relieved when their son or daughter is psychiatrically labelled or drugged, so that responsibility is taken out of their hands.

Skills of how to respond either to the aggressive or passive ways in which children exhibit underlying insecurities are vital to both parents' and children's welfare. Many of the challenges raised here are mirrored in the questions set out below. One of the key issues in responding to any challenging behaviours is to know that the behaviour presenting has meaning and is an attempt by the child to reveal some blocked need or inner fear. Reacting impatiently to the challenging behaviour will only increase it, because the focus of a parent's response needs to be on what lies hidden rather than on what is shown. This is not to say that when a challenging behaviour threatens the wellbeing of another, no action is taken. On the contrary, the challenging responses of one member of a family cannot be allowed to continue to threaten the welfare of the other members of a family.

Parents can learn much about their child's inner world and how best to respond by principally looking at the intention of the challenging behaviour and also to look at the causes. Patience is paramount when attempting to resolve family conflict. Important considerations are how frequently the challenging behaviour is occurring, how intense it is, how long it lasts when it occurs, and how long over time it has continued. Parents also need to remember that time changes nothing, without action. The notion that 'children grow out of their problems' is not accurate. Generally speaking, when trust has been lost in a family it takes considerable and consistent effort on the part of parents for children to feel safe and secure again. A further issue is that one child's challenging response is not the same as another's. The wisdom is to recognise that each child's signs of distress are unique and require and deserve a unique response from parents. Parents, too, need to realise that a solution that worked before may not be suitable when a similar challenging response appears in the future.

Parents have many questions around how best to respond to the challenging and often frustrating behaviours that children and young people show. Several of the most frequently asked questions in this area of children's behaviour are dealt with below.

## Q1. I FIND I LOSE MY TEMPER WHEN MY CHILD KEEPS ENGAGING IN AN ANNOYING BEHAVIOUR, EVEN THOUGH I HAVE REQUESTED SEVERAL TIMES THAT SHE STOP DOING IT. I FEEL GUILTY AFTER-WARDS. PLEASE HELP.

Five-year-old Mary is sitting at the table colouring with her crayons while her mother is studying for her university course. Mary begins to tap the crayon against the table. 'Please stop that, Mary,' her mother says crossly. Mary stops, but soon starts again. 'Mary, cut that noise out – I won't ask you again.' Mary stops again, but soon resumes the noise-making. Her mother slams down her book, reaches over and slaps the child, screaming 'I said stop that! Why do you keep doing it when you know it annoys me? Why can't you sit still and be quiet?'

It is clear from the above scene that Mary's mother is not having success in getting her need for quiet met; on the contrary, matters are escalating. The reason for this is that she is reacting to the child's irritating behaviour rather than attempting to understand it. To under-stand is a process of getting beneath the behavioural stance of self or another – in this case the child's tapping-the-crayon-behaviour.

Every behaviour has an intention; just as the mother's request for Mary to stop the noise has the intention of securing quiet so that she can study, so Mary's tapping behaviour also has motivation. Some writers believe that the child does not know, in spite of her mother's anger, why she is persisting with the annoying behaviour. However, I believe the child does know, but dares not express directly her hidden need for fear of rejection. Ingeniously, the child finds an indirect way of expressing her hidden goal.

In the scenario described above, neither mother nor daughter are clearly expressing their needs; indeed both are exhibiting distressing behaviours. It would help enormously if the mother sought to understand her own irritable response and expressed her need clearly. 'Mary, I need for you to be quiet so that I can concentrate on my study and finish it so that we can then have some time together.' It is ironic that the mother, in her exasperation, asks the child 'why do you keep doing it?'; the child could equally ask her mother 'why do you keep getting cross with me?' Communication is not at all clear between them.

It is important that the mother sees she is the main architect of the relationships that exists between her and the child. Children depend totally on their parents for love, nurturance, education and social and spiritual development. When there are any threats to these vital needs, children find creative way to reduce the threats.

If Mary's mother wants Mary to cooperate with her need for 'quiet to study', she needs to express it clearly and also attempt to understand the child's difficult behaviour. Unless we are aware of what lies behind a behaviour, we have little chance to secure the desired outcome. Only when the child's hidden need is identified, acknowledged and a commitment to meeting that need is made (where possible) can a change occur.

Sometimes the hidden purpose of a child's behaviour can be discovered by examining the results she obtains. Sometimes direct questioning may be too threatening, particularly when there has been a history of needs not being heeded. In looking at the results in the above interaction, the mother became annoyed. Mary wanted to annoy her for a hidden reason, and when her mother slapped her Mary secured her mother's full attention. Why would she stop? Look at the magnificent results! She can keep her mother occupied with her and no longer endure the emotional threat of being ignored. Mary's tapping noise is expressing accurately her feelings – 'Look at me! Talk to me instead of burying your nose in your books!' If her mother tapped into the child's need and if the child's quiet moments of constructive play brought a warm smile from her, a warm hug and a word of praise, the child would be far less inclined to get her attention through disturbing behaviour. Disturbing behaviour is a clever projection out from the child's mind and heart of her inner disturbance. By responding to the inner disturbance, Mary's mother will be effective in reducing its outer manifestation. However, she also needs to be in touch with her own inner annoyance and to do her best to respond to both the child's and her own needs. Children not only need to be loved but they also need to give love. Giving children the opportunities to be helpful, supportive and involved in the meeting of their parents' needs is essential to effective parenting. In the situation above, if the mother had requested Mary's support for her study and expressed her appreciation of the child's efforts to respond to the expressed need, the unpleasant scene between them could have been avoided.

## Q2. MY CHILD HAS CERTAIN BAD HABITS WHICH DRIVE ME WILD. NOTHING SEEMS TO WORK TO GET RID OF THEM. ANY IDEAS?

Some parents find certain behaviours of children very annoying and make the mistake of trying all sorts of tactics to eliminate the behaviours. Typical examples are thumb-sucking, nail-biting, masturbation, rapid eye-blink, facial tic and fetish behaviour (a child not willing to go anywhere or go to sleep without holding a particular object – teddy bear, piece of cloth). Using 'bad' words can also become a target for elimination. Those behaviours that can be viewed as troublesome by parents are often termed 'bad habits', but such a label masks their true meaning.

Children who present with such behaviours need help and understanding. The difficult behaviour is a symptom, a sign. Nothing can be gained by attempting to control the symptoms. Parents need to discover the underlying causes and then direct their attention to them. Observation of and casual and friendly conversation with the child are the means of arriving at understanding.

A parent may observe that the child thumb-sucks when tired or insecure or frightened. If the parent tries to stop the thumb-sucking by bribery, threats or putting a nauseous substance on the child's hands, the behaviour will only be increased. One of the reasons that the behaviour increases is that the symptom has been flown in vain and increasing its frequency and intensity is an attempt by the child to get the parent to look at the deeper issues. If the parent comforts the child when tired, builds up the child's sense of self or empowers the child around individuals or situations that are a source of threat, it is far more likely that the symptomatic behaviour will decrease and eventually disappear.

A child who nail-bites may be 'biting back' his anger, resentment and frustration about being over-controlled or continually criticised. Here again the distressing behaviour is a sign of the child feeling emotionally blocked; it is not a problem in itself. Again it is futile to punish, humiliate or prescribe preventative remedies. Parents cannot force the child to stop; they can only seek to remedy the cause.

When a parent attempts to force a child to desist from these 'nasty' mannerisms, the parent needs to ask herself: 'What is in me that is preventing me from being understanding and patient with these behaviours?' It may well be that the parent is embarrassed around these symptoms, but then this is a symptom that the parent needs to reflect on and discover its cause. A possible source of the 'embarrassment' feeling may be 'worrying about what other people think' or 'an over-intensity around cleanliness and hygiene' or a need 'to have everything looking perfect', including the child. What the parent needs to recognise is that the symptom of embarrassment is not the problem, but remedying its cause needs to be the target.

Parents need to be patient in their mature responding to a child's 'bad' habit. Many parents become discouraged if after a few weeks of attempting to remedy the cause, the symptomatic behaviour continues. An idea of the patience and time required can be gained by looking at the frequency and intensity of the behaviour, and how long it has been going on. Be optimistic and realise the creativity and intelligence of the child in the first place in creating the difficult symptom in order for you to see and remedy the deeper issues that are a source of threat to his or her security. Children need to know that we believe in their ability to overcome their fears and insecurities. In any case, a parent who becomes pessimistic and discouraged may need to look at her own level of belief in self. Remember, a parent can only give to a child what she has got herself. Very often the distressing symptoms present are an opportunity for all members of the family to reflect and liberate themselves from their fear and insecurities.

## Q3. HOW DO I MANAGE A CHILD/ADOLESCENT WHO IS OUT OF CONTROL?

A not unfamiliar scenario is a parent not dealing effectively with a teenager or child who responds aggressively to a 'no' or a request to do something. Sometimes the young person's verbal aggression can spill over into violence towards a parent or self or destruction of property. Some children or adolescents can keep up the onslaught for a lengthy time. The more 'out-of-control' the aggression is, the more difficult it is to deal with the situation calmly and effectively. Parents can be certain of three things:

- The purpose of the aggressive response is for the perpetrator to control the parent in order for him (or her) to get his or her own way.
- Aggression is not an acceptable means for any member of the family to gain any favourable response to a need.
- Responding to aggression with aggression is guaranteed to escalate the 'out-of-control' situation.

With regard to the first certainty above, the issue is emotionally weighted for the perpetrator and that has triggered the emotional and/or physical storm. However, in the immediate situation, the perpetrator is in no place to hear reason and it is counter-productive to attempt to discuss or argue the 'hot' issue. The response needed is one that will defuse the situation and very often that means saying nothing more and removing yourself from the perpetrator. After all, you have made your position clear or have declared a particular need. To continue to protest your situation not only weakens the conviction of your position, but it provides the perpetrator with a chink in your armour. More often than not you will be pursued and the pressure will continue. But aggression is like a fire – feed it and it will blaze all the more; stop feeding it and it will extinguish. So when pursued, maintain your 'no response' stance and address yourself to tasks in hand. Later on, when calm has been restored, it is advisable to enquire as to what led to such an unacceptable outburst. Do not assume that you know what is wrong with your son or daughter but, certainly, show concern about the level of upset they exhibited.

With regard to the second certainty above, there needs to be a very definite ground rule within the family that under no circumstances will aggression be tolerated as a means of interaction. What is accepted and encouraged is mutual respect and a communication that is direct, clear and which allows the receiver the freedom to say 'yes' or 'no' or 'I'll need to think about it'. Your child does deserve an explanation for a negative response.

The most powerful response to aggressive behaviour is to ensure that it does not achieve its end, which is control. Furthermore, because aggression violates the rights to respect and safety of parents and other siblings, some sanction needs to follow its manifestation. The purpose of the sanction is not to punish but to vindicate and restore the parent's violated rights. The sanctions can range from a request for an apology, to a deprivation of a privilege, to a reporting of the violation to an authority figure. It is vital that the sanction is imposed in a way that is respectful, non-punishing and meaningful. For example, 'I am not accepting being pushed by you because I deserve respect and safety. I am going to report this matter to your father. My purpose in doing this is to ensure no further violations of my rights'.

When applying sanctions it is mature to start with the least of the sanctions and, when necessary, work up to the most safeguarding of the sanctions. A sanction is only a sanction when it restores a violated right. Once the right is re-instated, no further reference to the aggressive action needs to be made. Some parents keep bringing up, like a broken record, incidences of aggression. Such threatening behaviour is bound to produce another hostile response.

The third certainty about aggression is that a defensive (rather than an assertive) response will aggravate the situation. However, it takes considerable maturity on the part of the parent to stay separate, firm and calm in response to a son's or daughter's aggression. Because parents perceive their child's response as a criticism or rejection of them, they feel hurt, and the tendency is to lash back. It helps enormously when parents can stay separate from their children's aggression and read the difficult behaviour as being 100 per cent about the perpetrator and not saying an iota about the receiver. The reason for each child's (or parent's) aggression is unique, but it is safe to say that some perceived hurt, rejection, misunderstanding or threat preceded the aggression. When the dust has settled and the parent has followed the procedures outlined above, the mature response is to provide as much safety and love as possible and to enquire as to what has hurt or threatened your son or daughter.

## Q4. MY CHILD IS SUCH A PERFECTIONIST. IS THIS A PROBLEM?

In clinical practice the children and adolescents that are most referred for help are those who are aggressive, disruptive, violent, hyperactive, apathetic and have lost motivation to learn. The second most referred group are children and young people who are shy, timid, fearful, school phobic, depressed and isolated. The children who are rarely referred are those who are perfectionistic, who put extreme pressure on themselves to perform academically (or otherwise), who cannot tolerate even positive criticism or direction and will avoid any challenges that they feel they would not be 'tops' in. These young people tend to fret and worry around examination times, tend to be emotionally and socially illiterate and often isolated from their peer group. Even though they are more emotionally and suicidally at risk than their aggressive, hyperactive or shy and timid peers, they are often the apple of their parents' and teachers' eyes. This is not surprising as they do not disrupt homes or classrooms and they bring home the prizes and achieve highly in the classrooms. Nonetheless, these children need as much, if not more, help as those students who are hostile to learning. However, whilst syndromes have been created to describe children with learning problems and drugs developed to control their difficult behaviour, I know of no such investigations into or psychiatric labelling of those children who are perfectionistic!

The signs of perfectionism are not too difficult to detect:

☐ Chronic fear of failure
☐ Addiction to success
☐ Long hours studying or working or practising
☐ Fear and fretting around examination or appraisal times
☐ Intolerance of even positive criticism
☐ Avoidance of challenges where others are likely to be better than them
☐ Dropping out from activities where their performance falls short of 'perfect'
☐ Social isolation
☐ Easily upset
☐ Thriving on success

Many children who are perfectionistic are often labelled 'gifted'. What is sad is that only 3 per cent of so-called 'gifted' children make any important social contribution as adults.

There is a major difference between children and adults who love and enjoy academic and other activities and those addicted to them; the latter are driven by fear and the former by challenge and adventure. The fears that drive those who are perfectionistic are fears of failure, criticism and rejection.

Perfectionism in children and adults is an addiction to success. The addiction to success is very powerful and it is difficult to overcome, because, unlike other addictions (alcohol, drugs, food, smoking), those who are success-driven are reinforced strongly for their over-dedication. Perfectionism in children can give them phenomenal academic (or other, for example, sports) success, status, praise and adulation.

Where there is addiction to success, self-worth and work are strongly intertwined and any falling short of a perfect performance can pose a serious threat to emotional and social wellbeing. The implication inherent in perfectionism is that 'without a perfect performance I am valueless and worthless'. It is for this very reason that children and adults are highly at risk – even a small drop in performance can plummet them into despair or dropping out from the activity that has been their means of proving themselves in the world.

I have helped children, adolescents and young adults who dropped out from school or university because they fell short of their perfectionistic standards. I have also seen young adults who showed amazing promise in a particular sport, but dropped out because of fear of not being able to maintain the high performance or because of a poor display.

Probably the saddest aspect of perfectionism is the absence of deep and unconditional loving relationships: success addiction can often be an emotional desert that must strike at the heart of those driven to succeed. However, if you are success-addicted and you decide to shift to giving priority to relationships, you risk the only acceptance and visibility you have known – the conditional recognition for successful performance in the 'desired' behaviour (academic or sports or domesticity or work, etc.)

Perfectionism is not a weakness, but it is a protection that seriously blocks a person's progress in life. Those who are perfectionistic have cleverly learned to gain visibility and recognition through their 'success', and this defence will be maintained until unconditionality is present – where the child or adult is cherished for self and not for what they do. The focus on helping those who are success-addicted needs to be on self-worth, not on the perfectionism. It is not wise to attempt to take a weapon away from anybody, but the need for a weapon disappears in the solid and safe world of unconditional love.

## Q5. MY CHILD SHOWS CONSIDERABLE AGGRESSION. HOW CAN I DEAL WITH IT?

I have always believed that one person's problems cannot be allowed to become another person's nightmare. This belief applies to both adults and children. It is now the legal situation that children who are at risk from parents or teachers or other adults are protected under the law. Physical, sexual, and emotional neglect of children is unlawful.

However, laws in themselves are rarely effective enough to bring about physical, psychological and social harmony. There are deep reasons why adults lash out at children and unless these are dealt with in an understanding and compassionate way, it is unlikely that individual maturity and social harmony will evolve.

Nonetheless, the law does offer some level of protection for children who are at risk. But what about adults who are at risk from children who are dangerous and verbally abusive? I know of many parents who suffer greatly at the hands of their children and for years teachers have been complaining about a rising tide of discipline problems. Indeed, many teachers who were good at teaching have left their jobs due to impossible discipline situations.

A recent benchmark decision by the High Court in London may pave the way for change in Ireland. The court ruled that 'teachers could not be forced to teach a disruptive pupil'. The teaching unions have welcomed the decision, insisting that their members must be protected from children who exhibit dangerous and/or abusive behaviour. A similar ruling is needed for parents who are at risk from their children.

Hopefully, any such ruling in Ireland would help to stem the exodus from teaching and lead to the creation of appropriate interventions for children who manifest aggression, particularly those children who have been excluded from school.

In England, the number of exclusions rose from 2,910 in 1991 to 10,400 in 1999. My guess is that the four-fold increase is mirrored here in Ireland.

Teachers and parents are not counsellors, psychologists, family therapists or social workers. For too long, teachers have been expected to cope with students who are disruptive. Regrettably, much of some teachers' own aggressiveness and use of cynicism and sarcasm arose from attempts to counter-control pupils who manifested disruptive behaviours.

Hopefully, the clear legal ruling means that neither teacher nor pupil will have to put up with such behaviours any longer and will lead to an improved classroom and school ethos.

While laws are desirable to provide safety to those who are at risk from the threatening behaviours of others, the laws do not resolve the reasons why children or adults act in ways that lessen the presence of others. There are many reasons why children show aggression; the reasons are often similar to children who are depressed, fearful, timid, perfectionistic, withdrawn and obsessive-compulsive. However, because these latter behaviours are not a source of threat to adults and other children, these children are tolerated in classrooms and homes. Nevertheless, these children require as much help as those who show aggression.

Possible sources of children's disruptive actions are: low self-esteem; insecure home situation; too much responsibility; over-protective parenting; pressure to perform academically; poor relationship with parents; open conflict at home; modelling of violence and verbal aggression by a parent; bullying by other children and/or by a parent/teacher; sexual abuse. The above list is not exhaustive; in any case, it is wiser to seek out the unique reason for each child's aggressive responses.

With real understanding, the reasons that are unique to a particular child may be revealed. Timing, patience and a willingness for adults to look to their own ways of relating to children and each other are essential. The issue of timing is important: there is no point in attempting to probe the reasons for the difficult behaviour when a child is shouting, screaming or hitting. It is essential for the adult to remain calm, not to personalise the outburst and not to attempt to control the young person. Only when the child has calmed down should the parent say, 'I really want to know what has upset you and what is it that you need.'

Certainly, such an attempt to understand must not weaken the resolve to ensure safety for those who are under threat. However, progress is much more likely to be made when parents, teachers and other adults work on both tracks – safety for selves and others, and understanding and action for the child who has perpetrated the disruptive action.

Issues of the frequency, intensity and endurance of the threatening behaviours are also important in determining the urgency and the nature of intervention that is needed to resolve young people's physical and verbal aggression and other disruptive behaviours.

## Q6. WHAT IS THE BEST WAY TO DEAL WITH A CHILD'S TEMPER TANTRUMS?

There are many parents who find themselves at the mercy of their children's temper tantrums. These temper tantrums can take the form of the child screaming, hitting, kicking, breaking things, holding her breath. Sometimes the outbursts can go on for hours. Not surprisingly, the patience of parents (and others) is sorely tested and, sometimes, 'for peace sake' they give in to the child or they lose self-control and become verbally or physically aggressive towards the child. Neither of these responses help the situation; indeed, both reactions only serve to escalate the frequency, intensity and endurance of the temper tantrums. When a parent 'gives in', this only serves to reinforce the intolerable way the child communicates. Likewise, to react aggressively is fighting fire with fire and serves only to inflame the difficult situation all the more.

Whilst it is easy to suggest to parents to stay separate from the temper tantrums and not personalise the child's blaming behaviours and 'I hate you' responses, in reality it is difficult to keep one's cool. Nevertheless, effort in this direction is essential for long-term resolution of the temper tantrums. What certainly helps is to not attempt to reason with the child when he is in such a highly emotionally charged state.

Emotion is always stronger than reason and the child is not in a place to respond to logic. Furthermore, action always speaks louder than words and a firm 'I'm not responding to your needs when you behave in this way' followed by a return to or an adoption of an activity and a determination to give no further verbal and non-verbal attention to the child's aggressive behaviour generally results in a de-escalation of the situation. Some children will pursue you and keep up the temper tantrum. The latter is often due to the fact that the temper tantrum has gained them what they wanted before and they are reluctant to let go of what worked previously. Their aim is to break your 'new' resolve and to regain 'power' over you. Naturally, the parent who is besieged in this manner needs to strengthen her resolve to stay separate, to not personalise and to continue to focus on whatever activity she has in hand.

Temper tantrums are common in two-year-olds – hence we talk about the 'terrible two's'. However, not all two-year-olds have temper tantrums! I believe that the frequency of temper tantrums at this early age is due to the rise in the number of 'no's' children begin to encounter and the resulting frustration in being blocked from pursuing their goals. The way adults say 'no' is important – it needs to be firm but not cross, consistent but not insistent, and always pre-dictable. Children require parents to have definite boundaries around certain behaviours and to maintain them when the child attempts to push the limits. Maintenance of mature limits creates security for children as they can depend on their parents to be strong in their caring of them. It does children's security no good when they are allowed to rule the roost.

Sometimes the purpose of temper tantrums is a subconscious attempt to correct a major imbalance in the exercise of power between a parent and a child. In a situation where a parent is highly passive and 'spoils' a child by giving her everything demanded, the child's exercise of overpowering this parent has the subconscious intention of getting the parent to exercise their responsibility and power as a parent and take charge of the untenable situation. The more the parent resists being firm, the more the child escalates the aggressive behaviour. 'Giving in' does not reduce temper tantrums, but being firm does. Firmness means maintaining your love for the child and being very definite that the temper tantrum will not gain the child her desired goal. Children's security rests largely on parents' strength of resolve and mature responding.

Another possible source for ongoing temper tantrums is the child whose parent aggressively overpowers him and deprives him of any sense of power. In this relationship the child's temper tantrums are designed to correct the imbalance of power by digging in his heels and refusing to cooperate with the overbearing parent. All control is about self-control and an important aspect of parenting is providing children with choices so that they can learn self-control of their behaviour. Parents who dominate or over-protect deprive children of this essential aspect of mature development.

There are parents who, at times, can feel utterly powerless in the face of their child's temper tantrums. Indeed, sometimes, the parent can feel hatred for the child and this often results in tremendous feelings of guilt when the storm is over. Such feelings are more likely to arise in situations where there are strong competing needs, like having to get to work on time, or get the other children out to school or get the child who is being difficult to go to the doctor or dentist and so on. In such situations, parents need to be understanding of and compassionate towards themselves in accepting how difficult parenting can be at times. In the event of their giving vent to such intense feelings, it is desirable that they apologise to the child. Furthermore, when temper tantrums persist, regular talking with (not at) children about what drives them to behave in that way, what their needs are and an honest expression by parents of their own frustration and needs will usually throw light on what further actions are needed to bring about family harmony.

## Q7. WHAT CAN I DO WHEN MY CHILD CREATES AN EMBARRASSING SCENE IN THE SUPERMARKET?

What is seen as difficult behaviour by children in super-markets, restaurants and other public places has become so common that in many cases it is accepted as normal. People, other than the beleaguered parent or childminder, whose tranquillity is disturbed, find it difficult to voice their discomfort for fear of being seen as not liking children or for fear of getting into conflict with or adding more to the stress of the child's guardian.

As adults we know, for example, that the supermarket is not a playground. The trouble is that children do not see the world through adults' eyes and for them the supermarket offers all sorts of play and pleasure possibilities. It is not that children want to make life difficult for adults but, never-theless, that is how adults typically perceive a situation where a child makes a chariot out of the shopping trolley or throws a temper tantrum when he does not get his selected toy or sweets. What we have is a clash of needs, the child's needs to play or experience pleasure and the adult's need to shop. Like many adults, children will attempt all sorts of ways to get their needs met and who can blame them for that?

However, the issue is that they need to learn that the supermarket is not a place where this happens and only parents and childminders can help them to get to grips with that reality. It is not necessary to get cross or aggressive; indeed, in situations where conflict occurs over a clash between children's and adults' needs, the best recourse is positive action; the least amount of words the better. Certainly, before entering the supermarket the parent can say, 'Mary, the shop is not a playground. You may walk up and down the aisles with me and help me put the groceries into the trolley'. If Mary jumps up on the trolley or begins pulling things from the shelves, the parent needs to immediately lead her by the hand out of the shop and to the car. Staying positively cheerful she can say: 'The supermarket is not a playground, so I will return later and do the shopping on my own.' It may well be that the child will raise a storm as the parent takes her from the store: an unmet need comes hard to all of us!

It is important that the parent sticks to her guns, not allowing other shoppers' stares or critical facial expressions to deter her from her mature action. This is not easy, particularly when a parent has the most common addiction of all, which is to what other people think. Faced with a child who is screaming and rebellious or crying helplessly, such a parent can feel helpless about getting her need to be liked met. She may attempt to verbally pressurise her daughter into submission and finally make threats which she will not carry out anyway. Sadly, when words do not work she may resort to physical punishment, which does not teach the child anything, other than 'I'm a bad girl' or 'Mummy doesn't love me'.

When a child reacts in the above ways, it is best that the parent abandons her shopping at this time as the task of educating the child in appropriate social behaviour needs to take priority. With such firm behaviour she is showing Mary that supermarkets are for shopping and not for playing. She can follow through on this by going on the next shopping outing on her own, but on the subsequent one she can allow the child the choice of coming with her if she thinks she can help her with the shopping.

It is vital that parents resist the temptation to employ verbal threats – 'If you don't behave you will stay in the car' or 'I'll take you straight home' or, equally disastrous, 'If you're a good girl, I'll get you a special treat'. The latter ploy is bribery and it only leads children to being manipulative and not being unconditionally responsible. Also, going into the supermarket and reminding children of their past 'misde-meanours' is not a good idea. It is best to operate in the present. Children's responsible behaviours need to spring from coming to terms with reality and from respect and care for others and not from threats or from receiving goodies and treats. Of course children deserve treats, but these should not be contingent on certain good behaviours.

Experience is always the best teacher and this is as true for children as it is for adults. Incidentally, when parents find it difficult to educate a child about the reality of certain situations because of fear of how other people see them, they have a responsibility to take on the challenge of accepting themselves, so they no longer feel dependent on others in order to feel good. Parents can only bring children to the same level of maturity they have reached themselves.

## Q8. HOW CAN I GET THE CHILDREN TO TIDY UP AFTER THEMSELVES?

One of the most common complaints of parents today is having to tidy up after other members of the family, and it is not always children. It would appear that some children resent a parent demanding they tidy things away after them. Sometimes children's resistance spirals the more a parent demands order in the home. A moral dilemma can ensue for the embattled parent. The mature parent knows she cannot force her children (or partner) into respecting her need for order. Yet her respect for herself would appear to militate against her picking up after them, running after them and allowing them to put her into their service and doing their jobs for them.

How can the parent have her need for tidiness and cooperation met? There are four fundamental issues to be addressed in attaining her goal:

- No parent has the right to force others to meet her needs
- The acceptance that a demand is not a command
- The knowing that she has a right to make a request for tidiness
- When her request is not met, she can take action for herself

The first issue speaks for itself but many parents still hold on to the notion that they have a right to control their children. Certainly, parents are required to foster self-control in children; ordering children (or anybody) is a recipe for conflict.

The second point concerns the frequent confusion between a demand and a command. Even the way a demand is expressed can reveal the hidden belief that 'I have a right to control you', not to mind the stiff body posture, intense eye messages and menacing facial expression.

Parents certainly have a right to request any need, but they also need to keep in mind that the receiver needs to be allowed to exercise his right to say 'yes' or 'no' to the request. A lot more needs are likely to be met when you positively and cheerily make requests and do not go overboard with gratitude when you are met with a 'yes', or sulk, withdraw or become hostile when you are met with a 'no'.

When a parent's request is greeted with a 'no', it is vital she remains pleasant and friendly and not in any way punishing. You might well ask 'is she not selling herself out?' On the contrary, the parent is maintaining her own self-control because she realises that it is her need for the common areas in the house to be tidy and that she is responsible for her own needs. It is then up to her to take her own determined action to fulfil her own need for tidiness and, at the same time, allow the other family members to be responsible for their own needs. With this conviction, when the mother finds things belonging to others out of place, she may pick them up and put them away – not for them but for herself, because they bother her and are in her way. However, only she knows where things are, since she picked them up. Since the children or partner did not put their belongings away, how can they know where they are? This is not punishment or manipulation. The logical result of not putting something away is that you do not know where it is. The toys disappear and likewise yesterday's newspaper. Since dishes and mugs are not put away, she will not serve any food in the living room. All of these actions for self are done with positivity, humour and without hostility and without preaching or nagging.

There is a strong possibility that when those who are untidy discover that their disorder does not upset the parent who wants tidiness, they may decide that order is more rewarding. Furthermore, if their disorder results in the disappearance of items belonging to them, they may be more careful to put them away.

When reasonable requests by a parent (or child) for order in a home are consistently and grossly ignored, there is a deep disturbance in the relationship between parent and parent, or between parents and children. Sometimes the disorder in the house symbolises the more profound disorder in relationships within the family and in the self-esteem of family members. When this is the case, correction of the untidiness will not be affected by following the above recommendations. The parents, who are the family architects, need to develop a plan or seek help to resolve the disharmonious relationships.

## Q9. IF MY CHILD IS REFUSING TO EAT, WHAT SHOULD I DO?

The idea of letting a child go hungry is horrifying to many parents. Actually, it is unpleasant to be hungry, but it is hardly life-threatening, except, of course, in the case of young people who are anorexic or bulimic. But one missed meal now and again is not going to cause bodily harm and the discomfort may be effective in stimulating children to eat at the next meal. It is certainly a better alternative to the friction and lack of harmony between child and parent that can result from forcing or cajoling the child into eating.

Parents do not have the right to assume the responsibilities of their children, nor do they have the right to take the consequences of their children's actions. Those belong to the children. Certainly, it is the responsibility of parents to put food on the table, particularly for younger children, but it is not their responsibility to make them eat it. Children eat when they are hungry; when eating becomes a problem, generally speaking, it is not eating that is the problem, but something deeper is being manifested through the eating problem.

A three-year-old girl was presented to me with the words: 'She's not eating; no matter whether we punish or bribe her she will not eat.' The child had had every physical examination done to get to the 'cause' of her problem. However, whilst the cause is important to detect, the intention of the 'not eating' symptom is equally important. Both father and mother came with the child. I noticed that the father appeared very into his physical appearance and, going on intuition, I explored this avenue as a possible cause. I discovered he was quite fastidious about his food – he would only eat fish and all his food had to be grilled. His slimness and 'perfect' weight were obsessions for him; he did not have any extra layer of flesh on him. I wondered how he viewed the typical 'pot belly' of a three-year-old and discovered that he constantly teased her about it, saying, 'fatty, fatty, fatty'.

The father's disapproval, his 'modelling' of the 'perfect' body and his 'finicky' approach to food were the causes of the child's not eating. She wasn't eating because she wanted to lose her pot belly and be slim like her dad. The child was clever enough to identify with her father in order not to suffer further rejection by him. I encouraged the father to desist from teasing the child and also to look at his addiction to having the perfect body. Within weeks, the child returned to normal eating.

Eating sustains life. It is a normal function. There is nearly always a parent with difficulties when a child develops a feeding problem. It is children's business to eat. The parents (and other adults) need to mind their own business and not the child's. It is frequently the case that when a child has an eating problem the purpose is to keep parents busy with him or her. Parents need to first ensure that the child is getting enough attention from them in other more spontaneous ways. At the meal table it is best to simply 'let' the child eat. If he refuses, the parents need to maintain positive behaviour, refrain from verbal reminders altogether, remove the unfinished food from the table when everyone is finished and allow the child to find out what happens next – when we do not eat, we get hungry. At the next meal, and not before, fresh food is again put on the table. If the child still plays with his food and does not eat, nothing is said, friendliness is maintained at the table. If the child continues to play with the food, the plate is casually removed. There must be no threat of punishment and no bribe or reward (for example, sweets).

The child may complain of hunger an hour later and plead for 'Coke and biscuits'. The parent needs to reply kindly, along the lines of: 'I am sorry you are hungry. Dinner will be ready at seven.' The suffering inflicted by scolding and threatening is punishment because it is perpetrated by the parent. The discomfort of going hungry is not inflicted by the parent, but is the result of not having eaten at mealtimes.

A subconscious desire to control lies behind many parenting behaviours. And it is often this very authoritative control that children fight, particularly at mealtimes. When parents decide to let go of their need to control, the child no longer has anything to battle against, there are no benefits in not eating, and the child is more likely to regain his appetite. It may take a little time and it certainly demands patience, but any sign of impatience results in the battle lines being drawn again.

## Q10. I'VE TRIED EVERYTHING TO GET MY CHILD TO STOP NAIL-BITING, BUT WITHOUT SUCCESS. ANY SOLUTIONS?

Compulsive nail-biting is not only experienced as a passing symptom by children and adolescents, but adults themselves often can suffer for years from this extremely difficult-to-treat condition. Yet the psychological reasons for nail-biting are fairly well-defined, and recognising the links involved may be helpful to parents when this symptom appears in their children.

What is certain is that threats, criticism, cajoling, bribing or prohibitions do not work and are not desirable responses.

Metaphorically, nails are weapons and when children or adults bite their nails, and some do it 'right down to the quick', what they may be psychologically doing is 'biting back' their anger. Children who nail-bite may cleverly have learned how threatening it is to express their anger and so, symbolically, they 'blunt their own weapons'. The biting itself is compensating to some degree, in that it helps to use up some of that anger, yet it is directed exclusively against themselves: to direct it against the source of their anger (parent, teacher, sibling) would result in greater hurt.

The frequency, intensity and duration of the symptom are important considerations. When it is often done to such a degree that the flesh becomes torn and bloody and this has gone on for months or years, appropriate intervention is expedient. When these circumstances are not present, it may well be just a passing phase.

As suggested, childhood nail-biting may be a sign that the child concerned realises that it is not emotionally, socially or physically safe to express his honest anger. Parents need to examine what their typical reactions are to anger in themselves, from their children and from others. A parent who is passive around their own feelings of anger does not model the appropriate and necessary expression of anger. Anger is a feeling, an energy that mobilises an adult or child to voice injustices, unfairness, blocked needs, nepotism, feelings of rejection, threat, tension and so on. People tend to confuse anger with aggression. Anger is a feeling and cannot hurt anyone; aggression is an action – verbal or physical – and can engender great fear, depending on how frequently and intensely it occurs. It is an overwhelming experience for children to encounter aggression from adults, particularly parents, teachers, relatives and other siblings. Ironically, aggression does not model for children how to assert their needs and feelings; indeed, it often leads to children learning to 'bottle up' their feelings, particularly anger.

In helping children to overcome their compulsion to nail-bite, you need to focus not on the nail-biting itself, but on the intention of the nail-biting, which is for the child to block his anger feelings. The provision of emotional, social and physical safety is central to helping children to express their inner lives, and, particularly, their anger. Emotional threats come in the form of a cross facial expression, threatening body-posture, warnings of 'don't be impertinent' or 'stroppy little fellow, aren't you?' or laughing at a child's efforts to express anger. Social threats occur in the presence of others and effectively take the form of putting down the child publicly for his assertiveness. Physical threats are those which directly physically punish children when any attempt to expose anger arises.

Children need the emotional encouragement, the social acceptance and the physical safety to express their honest anger and frustration. The most powerful means of helping children to spontaneously express their anger is by parents and other significant adults modelling the appropriate expression of anger. Mature expression of anger comes in the form of an 'I' message, for example, 'I feel angry when you put me down in front of people and I'm requesting respect and tolerance at future social functions'. When the targetted person does not meet your request, then use your anger for the action of asserting yourself in the public situation or choosing to walk away with dignity from the untenable situation. The important lesson that children need to learn is that their feelings of hurt and anger are not a justification to hurt and control others – which is what aggression (not anger) is all about.

Children's nail-biting will decrease as they practise mature expression of their feelings of anger.

## Q11.  ISN'T A CHILD WHO IS CONSTANTLY SEEKING ATTENTION JUST A PLAIN NUISANCE?

A frequent complaint of parents and teachers is that a child is 'an annoying attention-seeker'. Typically, the labelled child is highly demanding and wants attention centred upon her and her alone. Whenever anybody else is receiving attention, this child will escalate her efforts to get attention back to her.

When adults label a child (or adult) 'an attention-seeker', they would do well to recognise that there are good reasons why a child acts in this way and attention to those under-lying issues is crucial to resolving the child's unhappiness. Parents and other adults need to avoid being entrapped into conflict with the child.

What is certain is that children who seek constant attention are unhappy children. They have a deep insecurity about not being loved and wanted for themselves or not being free to be separate from their parents. Their attention-seeking behaviour is both a cry out for the emotional security of unconditional love and a protection from anonymity. The problem is that there is no real understanding of their longing, as parents tend to get irritated, frustrated and, sometimes, aggressive with the attention-seeking behaviour. Any of these responses convinces the child even more that he is not loved and there is a spiralling of his difficult behaviour. Some parents may 'give in' to the child's demands, but are at a loss to know why their patient responsivity does not reassure the child of their love. Very often the difficulty here is that the child is the one who gets the parents to go to him, but they do not spontaneously go to him. Sometimes, too, there may be an inconsistency in the parent's response, so that they are patient in one situation, but not in another.

You might well ask why does a child persist where the responses are frequently of a punishing nature? The answer to this question is that 'attention, even of a punishing nature, is still attention'. For a child who experiences little or no spontaneous attention from his parents, the pain of total invisibility is considerably greater than being punished by his parents.

Do parents have to put up with endless attention-seeking? The answer has to be 'no', but how parents convey the not being available at certain times and places is central to helping their child become secure. Take a situation where the mother is on the phone and the child continually nags her to do something for him. Staying separate from the child's attention-seeking behaviour is fundamental to addressing the child's hidden insecurity: the child's behaviour is about the child and not the parent. When a parent personalises the child's behaviour as the child deliberately being out to annoy her she fails to stay separate. Getting enmeshed with the attention-seeking behaviour generally leads to ill-temper and blaming of the child. Such a reaction serves only to reinforce the child's hidden insecurity and leads to an escalation of the attention-seeking behaviour. When a parent manages to stay separate she sees the troublesome behaviour as a revelation of the child's insecurity and welcomes it as an opportunity to deepen her relationship with the child. Staying separate, and showing understanding, patience and positive cheerfulness are the essential responses required.

There is a notion in behavioural psychology that when a child exhibits an attention-seeking behaviour, this is not the time to show interest in him. However, I believe this is the very time when he needs his parents' attention.

The mother on the phone is best to explain briefly to the caller what is happening with the child, ask for a few minutes to deal with the situation, put the phone down and go to her child and positively tell him she loves him, give him a hug and request that he not interrupt her talking on the phone. When she returns to the phone she needs to be determined to follow through on the phone conversation, throwing a look of appreciation for his cooperation. When he continues to act up, her best policy is to keep her total focus on the telephone conversation and give no energy or further response to the child's attempt to get her away from the phone. After the phone call she makes no reference to his attempts to interrupt but goes to him and tells him she loves him and invites him to help her with some domestic activity.

Children need and deserve our attention. Parents who over-attend and over-protect their children invite attention-seeking behaviour as children rightly surmise that is what their parents want of them.

## Q12. I'M CRACKING UP WITH MY CHILD'S CONSTANT WHINING 'I WANT, I WANT, I WANT'. IS THERE ANY-THING I CAN DO TO STOP THIS WHINING?

How many parents put up with a child whining or screaming 'I want it, I want it, I want it' and give in to the child's unreasonable demands for the 'sake of peace and quiet' or so as not to appear as 'a bad parent' in the eyes of others or out of some misguided notion that a child's needs must always be given in to. Sometimes the latter notion can be an attempt by the mother to compensate for the situation of a child being cheated out of having an at-home father because of separation or divorce. Some parents literally 'spoil' children and then wonder why they have difficulty in tolerating frustrations and taking on responsibility for their own lives as young adults. Parents have a major responsibility to acquaint children with the reality that not all their needs can be met due to limited resources, or fairness, or some needs having priority over others.

When a parent has difficulty in saying 'no', she shows not only a lack of respect for herself but also for the child. Sometimes the parent who pleases can also show lack of respect for order and for the needs of other adults who are exposed to and have to listen to the child acting out until he gets his needs met. Parents might be astonished if they were to count the number of times they give in to 'just this once' demands. It is a real act of caring when children are guided to see that each person in the family has needs and that cooperation between all members of the family is required to meet each person's needs whenever possible.

The consequences of pleasing children at all times can seriously limit their ability as children, and later as adults, to form secure relationships with others. Children who are spoiled have been led to expect that their needs are all-important and that the needs of others do not count. Their ability to develop cooperativeness is undermined. When they cannot have their own way they make everyone's life miserable. They have not learned how to be considerate, to tolerate frustration and delayed gratification and how to accept 'no' positively. The sad outcome is that when children who are spoiled meet situations in life where no one is concerned with pleasing them, they can feel helpless, let down and can experience deep depression. It is under-standable that the short-term harmony resulting from giving in to children blinds parents to the long-term consequences. However, mature parenting means preparing children for the inevitable frustrations that will arise in adult life. It is sheer neglect to assume that children will be able to meet frustrations when they are older. Toleration of frustration needs to start in the early years, especially during the 'terrible two's' year, and be maintained all throughout childhood and adolescence. Routine, order, cooperation, fairness and mutual respect require parents to say 'no' in positively cheerful ways so that children learn how to be cooperative in relationships and how to tolerate frustration.

Many children can respond violently to a parent's 'no'; nevertheless the parent's responsibility is to maintain order and respect for self and others. However, when a child is attempting to gain his own way through aggression or intense sulking, the time for reasoning with the child is not now opportune – emotion is always stronger than reason. What is required is positive and firm action that indicates that the 'no' response is going to be maintained. There is no need to argue with the child; repeat the 'no' once more and then go off about your business and, no matter how much the child escalates his attempts to get his own way, no attention is given to those behaviours. This lack of response shows the child that when you say 'no' you mean 'no'.

When a child has calmed down it is important to acknowledge his resentment by letting him know that it is frustrating not to have a need met and to explain why this has to happen at times. Ridiculing his temper outbursts or sulking does not demonstrate understanding, and the child is likely to feel hurt and guilty for his expressions of frustration.

Pleasing children as much as possible arises from insecurities within parents that they need to address before they are ready to achieve a balance between saying 'yes' and 'no' to children's demands. Worrying about what other people think or having an over-involved relationship with a child (due to a poor belonging to self) or living your life through a child are just some of the deep emotional issues that may need to be addressed.

## Q13. I FEEL HELPLESS WHEN MY CHILD CRIES. CAN YOU HELP?

Over the years as a therapist I have helped individuals who, in spite of witnessing horrendous situations of famine and war, children dead on their dead mothers' breasts, bodies torn apart from bombs, were unable to cry. It is not that they did not feel profound sadness; it was that no tears came to their eyes. Inevitably, the source of their dry eyes lay in experiences in childhood where their crying was severely punished. They wisely learned to 'bottle up' their tears, as any sign of weeping meant the threat of being viciously rejected by either their father or mother. No wonder their suppression of their tears was so powerful.

Not all of us have had extreme experiences such as these, but most men and indeed some women have considerable difficulty in shedding a tear, especially in public. They feel that to cry is to be weak and, like the song says, 'a little tear (can) let me down'.

Like adults in so many ways, children take their cue from their parents and peer group. Parents can have the defensive belief that it is wrong to cry in front of their children. They hide their tears, disguise them as a sniffle or dilute them with 'amn't I a big softie' and can also protectively believe that to cry in front of children is to unfairly burden them with adult concerns. Actually, the contrary is true, as the 'dry eyes' of parents result in children not wanting to burden their parents with their tears. It is frequently the case that what parents put out there about certain behaviours is what they get back.

In general, adults tend to shy away from crying and show uneasiness with tears. Rather than staying calm and showing empathy and compassion, many adults tend to cajole the person who is crying in a way that stops their tears. Adults who shy away from tears have lost the realisation of how tears are a wise way to release physical tension and emotion and lead to mature action being taken for the upsetting issue. Where children are concerned, it is the adult in charge who needs to take action on the child's reasons for crying.

There are even more subtle ways in which being tearful is punished: censoriously giving a tissue, or telling the person 'don't be upsetting yourself' or 'your parents will be upset if they see you cry' or 'come on, dry up those tears and let's see a smile'.

What men most fear is to be laughed at and many men expect that if they weep they would be laughed at. There are grounds for their fears, as there are for all fears, and a common experience for boys is to be mocked or laughed at when they cry. Girls, on the other hand, tend to have more permission to cry, but have been seen as the 'weaker sex' for doing so, especially by men. Not surprisingly, women can cry in front of each other, but are far more likely to hide their tears from men.

The first language that babies have is body language, and tears are employed cleverly by infants to show their needs and pains. Babies have different types of crying and the attentive adult can quickly decipher these and determine what the infant is attempting to communicate. Hunger, thirst, pain, loneliness, fatigue, fear and threat are some of the experiences for which an infant draws the attention of a parent or childminder. When these needs are responded to the baby will be soothed; when no change occurs it would suggest that further deciphering is required.

There is a school of thought that believes that babies who cry should not be picked up or responded to as this will only increase their crying. However, the opposite is true. While there are different kinds of crying, each kind has the purpose of revealing an unmet need. If the need is not met then it becomes necessary for the infant to escalate the tears in the hope that the hidden need will be spotted and served. Of course, if, in spite of crying, needs go unmet, the child may go into hopelessness, cease crying and lie still in their cots. Such a phenomenon was seen with many children in the orphanages in Romania.

In Java, infants rarely cry; this is due to the fact that their feet do not touch the ground for the first year as they are continuously carried by a member of the family. Because of the close bodily contact, the older child or adult carrying the baby can pick up earlier physical signs (particular movements such as heat, coldness, facial expression) that signal needs. In contrast, Western babies can cry an average of thirty minutes before being responded to.

Tears relieve tension and pent-up emotion and they also have the purpose of revealing an unmet need. When the latter is met – assuming it's reasonable – then tears dry up in the face of positive attentiveness to person and needs.

## Q14. NO MATTER WHAT I SAY OR DO MY OLDEST CHILD KEEPS DOING 'BAD' THINGS. IS THERE A REASON FOR THIS?

A not infrequent experience of parents is their first child becoming difficult, unmanageable, defiant, destructive and continuously getting himself into trouble following the birth of a second child. Such behaviour can be exacerbated when the new arrival is an exceptionally happy and responsive baby and continues in that vein as he grows older. Unwittingly, the parents may frequently remark 'how good' this child is and 'how bad' their older child is. The parents may have some sense that their older child is jealous of the baby, but may not see why, since they believe they are still devoted to him. However, parents need to understand matters from the child's point of view and see that their first child sees the new arrival as a usurper who has taken over the whole field of his parents' love and attention. Since his parents continue to be so impressed by his new brother's 'goodness', the eldest can give up entirely on the field of 'being good' and turn to 'being bad' in order to get his parents' attention. As the infant brother grows up and maintains his 'being good' as a way of impressing his parents, he will subtly get his older brother to fight with him so that he can put him into a further bad light, thus ensuring maintenance of his 'good' position. What is amazing is how both children manage to keep their parents busy with them, each in a different way. What is equally astonishing is how each child acts according to how he has perceived the family dynamics and, subconsciously, cooperates with the other to maintain the equilibrium and the competitive style. Some psychologists believe that the child who is being disruptive has misinterpreted the situation and that his younger brother is not being favoured by his parents. The implication is that the younger sibling has interpreted things accurately. I disagree; I believe both children have assessed the situation very well. The eldest child is no longer 'an only child' and his parents are exhibiting an over-responsiveness to the 'good' and 'compliant' behaviour of their second child. How can he compete with that?

Furthermore, the love shown is conditional: 'good' behaviour gaining love and attention and 'bad' behaviour earning criticism and rejection. However, what the parents are not realising is that in the eyes of their older child even a 'critical response' is attention. He prefers being scolded to being ignored. Contradictory as it may sound, the older child desires to be 'bad' because this serves his need to establish a place for himself within the family. 'I am the "bad" child. My parents are at a loss to know what to do with me. Herein lies my significance.' It is equally important to see that the youngest child has assessed the situation and has concluded: 'I am the "good" child. My parents are so pleased with me. Herein lies my significance.' However, both children will continue to experience deep insecurity.

The parents of these two children are in quite a dilemma. How can they encourage their older child to let go of being 'bad' and, even more so, how can they encourage their younger child to let go of having to be 'good'? The latter challenge is more difficult because the parents certainly do not want another 'difficult' child on their hands. The crux of this situation, and this applies to both children, is that a child is not his behaviour. All children, just like adults, exhibit a mix of 'good' and 'bad' behaviours, but it is the unique presence of each child that deserves and needs love, celebration, cherishing and acceptance. No 'difficult' behaviour, or indeed 'pleasing' behaviour, merits the withdrawing or giving of love respectively. Certainly, a difficult behaviour needs to be positively, lovingly and cheerfully corrected, but in a way in which the child sees that it is the 'specific' behaviour that is being corrected and not him. This is true also for the 'good' action; that attention is given to the 'specific' action and not the child. For example, when a child is being defiant, the parent may say 'John, I need the toys to be tidied away please; come on, let's do it together. To respond to a child's defiance with 'You're a bold boy' is an act of rejection and the child interprets this response accurately. Similarly, when a child tidies away his toys on request, the appropriate response is 'Mark, thank you for tidying away your toys.' The conditional and more common response is 'Mark, you're such a good boy.'

Each child has the deepest longing for his or her unique presence to be affirmed and for their actions to be specifically encouraged but not mistaken for their person.

## Q15. MY CHILD REACTS BADLY TO BEING TEASED: ANY IDEAS WHY?

Teasing can be benign in nature or it can have a cutting edge to it. Most people are not too bothered by benign teasing, even though children can react badly to what parents often perceive as a playful response to a child's engaging mannerism. The difficulty here is that the child feels exposed and is not sure what he's done and feels embarrassed and awkward. To a parent's consternation, the child may cry, sulk or get aggressive, the subconscious intention being to get his parents to stop the teasing.

Whether it is a child or an adult who teases, the teasing is always about the person who teases. Likewise, when the person who is the target of the tease reacts, the reaction is about him or her. Clearly, when teasing is an underhand way of 'sticking the knife in', there is some serious issue that those individuals who tease need to address in themselves. Similarly, when people react to being teased there is a hidden challenge for them to discover. The more intense the reaction, the greater the challenge.

Teasing between adolescent boys (or girls) can, sometimes, have a vicious quality to it. The adolescent who teases targets a vulnerability in his peer and goes for it. However, what lies hidden is that the teaser himself is terrified of manifesting that vulnerability (say, crying or being fearful), and in putting down the other boy for displaying such a behaviour, he takes the limelight off himself and reduces the possibility of exhibiting this taboo behaviour himself. Woe betide anyone who exposes his hidden fear. The challenge for these boys is to admit what they feel.

Teasing is quite common on sports fields, because losing in our culture has become associated with ridicule and put-down. The intention of the losers' teasing of the winning team – 'a crowd of teachers' pets' or 'a team of gits' – is to soften the blow of defeat and deflect blame from themselves. The hidden challenge here is for young people to embrace failure and free themselves of the addiction to what other people think.

When it comes to adolescent boys and girls, the purpose of the tease is not difficult to see, especially when it comes to the time when boys begin to become romantically and, later on, sexually attracted to girls and vice versa. It is a con-siderable capitulation for adolescent boys to admit to an attraction to girls from a position where up to then they saw girls as 'silly, soft and babyish', or indeed for girls, who saw boys as 'rough, uncouth and boorish'. The tease is a masked means of expressing an attraction, which can be quickly withdrawn by 'I was only fooling' should the teasing not have the desired result of mutual attraction.

Teasing between adults can be a clever ploy to address an issue that is too threatening for the person teasing to address directly – for example, body odour or meanness or aggression. Teasing affords you the means of communicating a message in an unclear though witty way, without having to directly and clearly confront the person exhibiting the troublesome behaviour. Individuals can defensively fool themselves by saying 'I'm using the tease so that I don't hurt the person's feelings', but the reality is that the tease protects the teaser from possible hurt or rejection. The challenge for the teaser is to be open about his or her needs and stay separate from the person's reaction.

When adults react to a tease with embarrassment, aggression, sulking, cynicism or sarcasm, they have internalised the teasing message as being about themselves, rather than recognising that the tease is 100 per cent about the teaser. Learning to hold on to one's own sense of value and beliefs may be the challenge that lies hidden behind the reaction. A proactive response to the teaser would be 'I'd really like to know what is the real message you want to send.'

Sexual teasing between adults can be distinctly unpleasant and always reveals a sexual and emotional immaturity on the part of those who tease and those who react. Those who tease do not have the personal confidence to express their needs directly and clearly. Those who react tend to respond with an equally nasty sexual tease, but they need to be quick on the defense to do that and be ready to deal with the hostility that often lies hovering behind the sexual tease. However, unless we tease back in a way that does not put down the teaser, no change will occur in this fundamentally hostile kind of teasing. Both teaser and teasee remain stuck in their doubts about themselves.

## Q16. WHY DOES MY CHILD CONSTANTLY LIE?

A common complaint from parents about their children is 'she is always lying to me'. Some parents are surprised by my response of 'why isn't it safe for the child to tell the truth?' The hidden purpose of a lie is not to deceive but to offset hurt and rejection.

Children will tell the truth when it is both emotionally and physically safe to do so. When there is any hint of a threat, they will wisely withhold the truth. Some parents and teachers put the Gestapo in the halfpenny place when it comes to interrogation. Intuitively children assess the risks of judgement, ridicule, punishment and rejection and resort to the protective power of lying. Safety is created by a positive cheerfulness, a non-judgemental attitude, the presence of love and regard and the demonstration of understanding and compassion: 'John, I understand there may be reasons you took money from my purse and I am concerned to know the truth so that we can work together so that it does not happen again.'

Whether you are communicating to a child or an adult, there are always two aspects to your message – the verbal and the non-verbal. Children always respond to the non-verbal message. Whilst the verbal message given above is open and mature, if it is said crossly or anxiously or with a feeling of disappointment, the child will detect the threat and more than likely lie. However, when there is congruence so that both the verbal and non-verbal messages are saying the same thing, the child is likely to tell the truth. Sometimes the reassurance of understanding and non-judgement may need to be repeated a number of times before the child feels safe to own up to what he has done.

The commonest kind of lying children engage in is around exaggeration of reality. 'My dad is ten times stronger than your dad'. Having bigger and better parents, or a huge stamp collection or having the most amazing monsters visiting him are some examples of this type of lying. The reality may be directly opposite to the lies and so the child is cleverly compensating for his feelings of insecurity and fears of not being good enough in the eyes of others. The child is attempting to show how little he feels and it is important that parents and teachers help this child to feel better about himself. Clearly, how often the child tells the stories, how tall the stories are and how long over time this kind of lying has endured are important indicators of the level of the child's insecurity.

In couple relationships one partner can frequently complain 'I can't trust him; I can't believe a word that comes out of his mouth'. Sometimes the demand for trust springs from insecurity and doubts about your attractiveness or ability to hold a relationship. Rigidity around the demand for truth is a clever and covert means of reducing the possibility of ever losing your partner to another as you make sure you are in the know about his whereabouts at all times.

There is quite a difference between a request for truth and openness in a relationship and the demand for such transparency. The individual who makes a request will recognise that there are times when a partner may need to keep some aspects of his life private. For example, a diary is a private memoir of daily experiences and nobody has the right to invade that space. The person who demands that 'there must be no secrets between us' does not respect privacy; indeed, her partner's need for his own space and time will threaten her. The challenge for the person who cannot tolerate a lie is to find her security in herself and break the cycle of co-dependent relationships.

But what of the person who is a compulsive liar and frequently weaves an elaborate and colourful tapestry of lies? What can often lie hidden here is a poor sense of value in self. This man feels nobody would find him attractive and interesting and so he invents for himself an alternative persona and a life that involves danger and challenge. Lying is an act of creation, a way of filling the void within. The stories he tells are projections of emotional states – love, friendship, sexual intimacy – which he dare not allow himself to experience directly. Whilst his lying dulls some of his inner pain, it never resolves it. He needs professional help to access his real, unique, sacred and attractive self so that he will no longer need to live a masquerade.

## Q17. MY CHILDREN ARE CONSTANTLY FIGHTING WITH EACH OTHER AND IT'S DRIVING ME CRAZY! WHAT CAN I DO?

'For heaven's sake, stop that fighting, you're driving me crazy', the parent yells from another room. 'Michael won't let me watch my programme', James shouts back. 'I never get to watch what I want to watch', Michael roars in turn.

How many times do parents encounter the above or a similar situation, then get into trying to settle the dispute and end up not pleasing anyone.

Of course, parents feel upset and deeply concerned about the ceaseless fighting that can go on among siblings. They love each child, and it hurts to see the children you love hate and hurt each other. A great deal of parenting energy goes into settling fights and attempting to get children to get along together.

Many children eventually 'outgrow' fighting and come to a place of appreciation and care for each other. In some cases the hostility continues into adulthood, even to the grave.

Recently, I was somewhat dismayed to read a psychologist's recommendation that parents should stay out of children's fights, even where there is physical violence or major emotional and social lessening of each other's presence. Certainly, it is important to support children to resolve their difficulties themselves, but where there are differences in age, size and gender, a fair resolution is less likely to result.

I know of many families where an older sibling made the lives of younger siblings miserable and the parents did not intervene. Parents are the family architects and it is their responsibility to ensure that differences between children do not escalate to physical, emotional and social hurting of each other. It is inevitable in every family that differences emerge between children but how those differences are handled is the responsibility of parents. I am not suggesting that parents impose solutions, as this deprives children of the opportunities of learning to problem-solve.

Resolving conflict is an essential life-skill and the earlier in life it is learned the better. However, parents can only pass on skills they have got themselves. Furthermore, the most powerful way for parents to teach children to resolve their differences without resorting to hurting each other is by demonstrating how they resolve their difficulties with each other and with the children. Teaching children how to problem-solve needs to be not 'do as I say' but 'do as I do'. When children witness parents in conflict, shouting or hitting each other or engaging in sulking and silent treatment, they are likely to repeat these darkening ways of getting their own way. The contrary is also true – when children witness parents resolving their differences with respect, active listening and fairness, they are likely to repeat these mature processes.

Most fights between children are about a competition of needs; for example, each wants to watch a different programme; each wants to play outfield and nobody wants to play in goal; without requesting, one borrows the other's toys or clothes.

Certainly, it is not the business of parents to decide which child does what when there is disagreement between them. However, it is the responsibility of parents to ensure that certain ground rules are followed during the negotiation that is required for the children to resolve their differences. Ground rules are there to protect the dignity of each person in the family (and that includes parents). Essential ground rules are 'no hitting', 'no shouting', 'no threatening', 'no silent treatment' and 'no labelling'. Any of these responses, depending on their intensity, frequency and how long they continue in the immediate moment and over time, considerably demean the presence of the person at the receiving end of them. Each person in the family needs to be treated with respect, and communication between parent and parent, parent and child, and child and child needs to consistently reflect this family value. When ground rules are broken by children in their fights, it is crucial that parents step in and strongly remind the children that differences between them do not even remotely merit disrespect for each other. When a child does not respond to the request of the parent to desist from the demeaning behaviour, then some sanction is needed to bring home to the child perpetrating the physical or emotional or social violation of his or her sibling that such behaviour is not tolerated in this family. The purpose of the sanction (for example, loss of privilege) is to give sanctuary to the child whose right to respect has been violated.

Such an intervention by a parent is not an attempt to 'fix' the problem existing between the fighting pair, but it is an assertion of the sacredness of each person in the family. When applying a sanction, parents themselves cannot afford to lose sight of the ground rules, otherwise their words will cease to matter to their children. It is not wise to have double standards or one law for children and another for adults.

When peace has been restored, parents need to encourage the pair who were fighting to negotiate their differences whilst maintaining a climate of mutual respect. Parents can be at hand to offer support and, maybe, brainstorm possible solutions to their children's problems. However, the choosing and implementation of the chosen solution is the responsibility of the children, and it is here that parents need to mind their own business.

# CHAPTER FIVE

# HOW CAN PARENTS RESOLVE THEIR OWN CHALLENGING BEHAVIOURS?

## INTRODUCTION

This is something that some parents find difficult – to examine closely their own inner and outer lives and the ways in which they relate to children in terms of the self of the child and the several areas of human expression – physical, emotional, intellectual, behavioural, social, creative and spiritual. The parent's manner of relating to a child mirrors what aspects of self the child will continue to reveal and those qualities he dare not show. The most threatening challenging behaviour that a parent may have to face is the confusion of the child's self with his behaviour. Children, like adults, have an innate need to be cherished for self. When a parent labels the child as 'bad' when he presents difficult responses or 'good' when he exhibits attractive behaviours, the child will intuitively assess that it is his behaviour that is seen, but, sadly, not his unique self. Once this happens the door to the child's expression of his fullness becomes blocked depending on the frequency, intensity and duration of the blows to his presence.

Parents do not deliberately set out to block a child's self-realisation, but as pointed out several times already, parents can only bring children to the same level of self-expression they have attained themselves. This can appear as an awesome challenge for parents (and teachers) to take on, and for that reason it is not surprising to find a wide acceptance of the labelling of children as suffering from attention-deficit disorder (ADD) or with accompanying hyperactivity (ADDH) or dyspraxia or dyslexia or the new syndrome, oppositional defiance disorder (ODD), or other non-psychiatric labels such as shy, timid, fearful, stupid, bad, slow, average, evil, good, brilliant. This labelling does not result in any meaningful response being shown to the child's manifestation of distress. The percentage of children being put on drugs is frightening and demonstrates less and less support for parents to understand their own and their children's challenging behaviours.

It is imperative that parents know themselves. Every time they engage in a challenging response that casts a shadow on their child's presence, they are being invited to examine the message for themselves that lies in these responses. When a parent is impatient, fearful, aggressive, intolerant, short-tempered, perfectionistic, rigid, cynical, sarcastic, or sulks, berates, belittles, compares one child to another, shouts, over-protects or spoils, that parent needs to ask herself what all these challenging responses are saying about her present sense of self. Many of the questions posed below help the parent to trace the origins of her challenging behaviours and show the way to free herself of her blocks to her full expression of self.

Parents who are seriously or chronically depressed, anxious, obsessional-compulsive, anorexic, bulimic, delusional, hallucinating or addicted to drugs, alcohol, sex, success, company, gambling, etc., need to urgently seek professional help so that these deep-seated challenging behaviours do not become major blocks to their children's progress. The help they seek needs to be of a psychotherapeutic nature, as the common reliance on medication does not resolve the reasons why people act in the dark ways they do. The nature of these particularly distressing challenging behaviours are elaborated on in questions posed towards the end of this chapter.

## Q1. WHY DO I KEEP GETTING CROSS WITH MY CHILDREN?

I know that when I use cross words I am at sixes and sevens within myself and there is something happening that is a threat to my presence. The cross words are not designed to hurt, put down or demean the person(s) at the receiving end, but, nonetheless, this is their darkening effect. My purpose is to attempt to control the other person into not being a threat to my security. However, that is putting an unfair responsibility for my security onto another and it also maintains my dependency on another for recognition. It is important for both myself and the other person that I own my own vulnerability and seize it as an opportunity for personal and interpersonal development.

There are many possible precipitants to my becoming cross:

▫ Being shown up
▫ Failure
▫ Lack of appreciation
▫ Ignoring my presence
▫ Cynicism
▫ Sarcasm
▫ Verbal aggression
▫ Work pressures
▫ Exam pressures
▫ Somebody not turning up
▫ Birthday not being remembered

The list is potentially exhaustive, particularly when you are dependent on people and things outside of yourself to help you feel good. When you examine each of the precipitants above, it is very clear that your sense of yourself is enmeshed with what happens outside yourself. It is that very enmesh-ment that will trigger your cross reaction. Possible cross responses to the above experiences are:

▫ Put down the person who shows you up
▫ Blame failure on others or unfair examination system
▫ Command appreciation
▫ Verbally attack the person(s) ignoring your presence

- Counter-cynicism
- Be even more sarcastic than your opponent
- Fight verbal aggression with verbal aggression
- Complain about work pressures
- Express hostility to exams
- Read the riot act to the person who did not turn up
- Throw a temper tantrum in response to your forgotten birthday

Even though the purpose of the above responses is to make sure those things do not happen again or to reduce expectations, the problem is you diminish the person(s) you attack and you are not dealing with the underlying causes. Nothing will change and the cycle of your crossness in response to outside threats will continue.

Ironically, your cross responses to others often mirror your internal conflicts, and breaking the vicious cycle of cross words lies in focusing on those issues. In examining the two lists above, hypothetical internal causes may be:

- Poor self-esteem
- Fear of failure
- Dependence on approval
- Out of touch with own presence
- Dependent on how others see you
- Wanting people to like you
- Poor nurturance of self
- Enmeshment of your worth with work
- Getting recognition through success
- Not being there for yourself
- Not celebrating self

I am not at all suggesting that you show passive responses to behaviour or circumstances that darken your presence. On the contrary, I would wish that you strongly assert your worth in the face of any lessening of your presence. But the central issue is that you do not demean or lessen another person's presence because you are feeling vulnerable. The constructive and mature approach is to touch into your own sacred person and from that solid interior ground, to voice your worth and value and stay independent of people's responses to such maturity. Sadly, it is our light, not our darkenss, that can threaten others.

Mature responses to the list of precipitants given above could be:

- □  'I am happy to own my oversight on that matter.'
- □  'I can build on that failure.'
- □  'I appreciate my own efforts and can request (not command) appreciation from others.'
- □  'I am in possession of my own sacred person and can enquire "why am I being ignored here?"'
- □  'Cynicism is a revelation of the other person's vulnerability; it is not about me.'
- □  'I will assert my own beliefs and not be controlled with sarcasm.'
- □  'Out of respect for myself and the other I will not respond to verbal aggression.'
- □  'I need to get my priorities right around work.'
- □  'Exams are an experience and not a measure of my worth.'
- □  'I can ring and enquire why the person did not turn up.'
- □  'I can request my birthday be remembered.'

Communication is a difficult process but it helps enormously when you attempt to communicate out from the centre of your own immense worth.

## Q2. I KEEP TELLING MY CHILDREN 'FOR PEACE SAKE DON'T UPSET YOUR FATHER'; IS THIS PROHIBITION A GOOD THING TO DO?

The prohibition 'dont upset your father' is different to the prohibition 'don't upset your mother'. Generally speaking, not upsetting your father is a clever protective means of not provoking his aggression. I deliberately say 'aggression' rather than 'anger' because anger is a powerful feeling that cannot hurt anyone, but aggression is an action that can have devastating effects on those children and adults who are at its receiving end.

Anger is a feeling that gives you energy to mobilise your own intellectual, emotional and social resources to take responsibility for and action on any needs of yours that are being blocked or to safeguard any rights of yours that are under threat or are being violated.

Aggression is a verbal, non-verbal or physical action that attempts to force others to meet your needs. Depending on its frequency, intensity and persistence over time, it can trigger equally intensive reactions of terror, fear, passivity, suicide, counter-aggression and murder.

The 'don't cross me' prohibition is not just found in homes, but in classrooms, workplaces, communities and sports fields. For those who are in a solid and safe place to see, it can reveal a deep vulnerability to rejection, failure, loss-of-face or dependence on success on the part of those who per-petrate the aggression. Nevertheless, its effects can shatter the lives of children, spouses and families, and it can have adverse effects on communities and society in general.

When male aggression and dominance is present in homes, it is frequently the case that the female partner colludes with it by 'keeping the peace', over-pleasing, passivity and encour-aging the children to engage in the same sad protective ploy.

The result is that the only voice that is heard in the family is the father's. The inner voice of truth that is within each other member of the family gradually becomes weaker or totally silenced. Individuality and creativity are suppressed and the father's voice is not to be contradicted. The 'peace' that is attained through generating fear is a 'pseudo-peace'. No one in the family is at peace, least of all the father. Real peace needs to be the goal of all social systems wherein each member is valued, respected, treated as an equal and allowed to express his or her innate individuality and difference. This is true for couple relationships, families, workplaces, churches, communities, sports clubs and divided peoples.

The mother in a family held to ransom by the father's aggression has a responsibility to herself and to her children to find the help and support to confront her partner's dark behaviour. Thankfully, more and more women are asserting their right for real peace in relationships. However, in some situations the risks can be great, not only to the woman, but also to the children. It is for this reason that the social and legal structures to protect people from emotional and physical intimidation have to be strong, accessible and compassionate. Too often such structures fail in their social brief.

The father who wields the weapon of aggression has hidden fears, even terrors, and, subconsciously, needs someone to confront his untenable behaviour. Like us all, he needs to be seen and valued for himself, but he seriously doubts his worthiness. He requires help and support to resolve his co-dependency with his partner, children and others. Such a process is only possible when he begins to accept his protective aggression as a means of immature control of others and to access his own worth and sacredness.

While couples are likely to form a co-dependent liaison, it is not often acknowledged that parents too tend to create a co-dependency with their children. So, the father who aggressively controls his children to conform to his ways and values is dependent on them for recognition. In order to survive, the children wisely yield to his control and, more often than not, continue not to do anything without their father's say-so, right into adulthood, sometimes even into old age. Some children rebel during their adolescent years and get into the battle of counter-control strategies. There are young people who may physically and verbally 'beat-up' the parent who mistreated them. It is in this context that the saying 'like father, like son' has poignant meaning. However, the young person's rebelliousness maintains the co-dependency, as the aim is still an attempt, through aggressive means, to gain recognition from the father who did not see the young person for himself. Thus the cycle of aggression is perpetuated, not because of genetics, but because nobody within the family, across the generations, has resolved the source of aggression.

Salvation for those young adults who have been victims of an over-powering parent is to break the cycle of co-dependency by moving towards in-dependence, wherein security comes from celebration, acceptance and love of self. When you find the solid ground of your own vast and sacred interiority, nobody can exclude, exile, demean or lessen your presence. You are also in a place to see that the aggressive responses of your father (and others) are revelations of his darkness, and because you are no longer the dependent child, you can hold onto the light of your precious presence.

Salvation for children entrapped with a father who employs aggression rests with the other significant adults in their lives to take the actions required to confront the threatening situation and protect children from violations of their physical, emotional, social and spiritual rights.

## Q3. CAN I LOVE MY CHILDREN TOO MUCH?

Love is a two-sided coin: it is about both the giving and the receiving of love. In general, women tend to be very good at showing love but poor at receiving it; on the other hand, men are masters at receiving love but novices at demonstrating it. Hence women, who are the 'givers', people the professions (nursing, teaching, parenting, counselling, social work) that demand the ability to nurture others; and men, who have been reared to be the 'takers', go into the professions (science, legal, construction, business) that are concrete, logical and non-emotionally demanding.

What is sad is that men have locked inside themselves the need to give love, and women have imprisoned their innate need to receive love. For men to risk showing love and for women to risk receiving it means going against the culture that still defines very polarised roles for men and women.

When the polarisation is extreme, women become addicted to giving and men to taking. Effective relationships are about 'give and take', and this two-way street ensures that the needs of both parties in a relationship are voiced and more often than not met.

The woman who has a compulsive drive to care for others rarely considers herself. She tends to be more concerned about helping others and never expects anything in return. Indeed, any attempt to give to a person who is locked into caring will be countered by embarrassment, protests of 'don't be wasting your money on me' or 'you shouldn't have done that' or 'haven't you enough to be thinking of'. Even more revealing is the attempt to block somebody who compulsively cares from doing things for you. Indeed, it is more difficult to take a caring behaviour away from this person than it is to take a drink or drug away from persons addicted to alcohol or drugs. The response to 'I can manage by myself' will be met by sulking or withdrawal or 'you don't want me in your life'. Very often 'for peace sake' you give in and allow the caring to continue; this reaction is neither good for you nor for the person who is driven to care. It means the addictive cycle will continue and the relationship remains one-sided for both parties, she to give and he to take.

Not surprisingly, relationships that are one-way eventually break down. The person who cares is often overwhelmed when a partner or son or daughter attempts to break away. She feels 'how could they do this after all I've done for them'. Sadly, what she does not realise is that constant doing for another renders the receiver helpless and, most importantly, blocks him (or her) from the privilege of exhibiting love. Helping is not about doings things for others; rather it is about giving people skills so that they can do things for themselves. What people addicted to caring often fail to see is that their kind of helping is profoundly arrogant because in effect what the person is saying is 'I know what's best for you'. Persons who are addicted to caring find it extremely difficult to let others be free to make their own decisions and mistakes. Most of all they make it difficult for them to demonstrate love.

Women and men who are addicted to helping others subconsciously believe that if they are always helpful, others will need them and therefore like them more. They do not have a sense that they are worthy to receive love (only to give it) and so they undervalue themselves and allow themselves to be taken advantage of.

The turning point that is required is a recognition of the addictive pattern, the development of a sense of self that is deserving of both the giving and receiving of love, a valuing of one's own needs and the creation of a balance between giving and receiving. As for all addictions, help, support and patience is needed to reach a state of wellbeing.

## Q4. WHAT EFFECT DOES THE PROHIBITION 'FOR PEACE SAKE DON'T UPSET YOUR MOTHER' HAVE ON CHILDREN'S WELLBEING?

The meaning behind the prohibition 'don't upset your mother' is different to what is meant by 'don't upset your father', which was dealt with in Question 2. Over the years there have been many individuals I have helped who initially presented with fears of upsetting others, passivity, guilt and an extreme eagerness to please. The source of such blocks to the full expression of self lies in childhood experiences, not least the unwritten rule that exists in many families: 'For peace sake don't upset your mother'. How does it come about that the vulnerability of one parent can control all the other members of the family?

The mother who does not cope with upsetting events may exhibit all sorts of distressing reactions when the rule is broken. Possibilities are withdrawal, inconsolable crying, fainting, histrionic responses ('you'll be the death of me'; 'what have I done to deserve this'). The mother is often the parent who does everything for her offspring and spouse, but there is a string attached and that is you have to go along with the way she sees the world. Even when the children are adults and may be married with their own children, there are frequent, if not weekly get-togethers of the entire family plus sons and daughters-in-law. Nobody dare say 'no' to these invitations. Christmas and New Year celebrations are also held in the home of the family of origin. Anybody – blood or in-law – who dares to ignore these obligations is firmly and acidly ostracised. The problem is not seen as the rigidity of the mother, but the ungrateful behaviour of the person who rebels. Only good news must be brought to this mother and all sorts of secrets and 'hush hush' litter the history of this family.

By conforming to the mother's vulnerability everyone loses out. The children tend to learn their lessons well from their father who colludes with his wife's vulnerability. Children have no model within the family to break the taboo and the situation that existed for them as children tends to be repeated when they marry and have children. There is a strong delusion here that 'my parents were such wonderful parents and it would be ungrateful of me to say anything even bordering on criticism'.

The fact is that your parents are wonderful persons, but that does not mean they were effective at parenting. Parenting is a difficult and complex profession, but there are few parents who enter the profession without some emotional, social, sexual, physical, occupational and spiritual baggage. Whether parent or spouse or lover or colleague or manager or entre-preneur, each adult has a responsibility to resolve (or at least be in the process of resolving) their immature beliefs and behaviours.

There is no intention here to blame the mother who cannot be upset or, indeed, the father who yields to such a limitation. There are sound reasons why each parent adopts such protective roles, but the consequences are dire for their own as well as their children's progress in life. The 'martyr' parent may well have learned as a child to keep conflict between her parents at bay or keep a vulnerable parent happy by pleasing him or her all the time. The problem is that the child never learns to deal with conflict and to see conflict as being necessary and creative to the deepening and maturing of relationships. How can a mother ever get to know her children when they have learned to 'bottle up' their hurts, anger, fears, ambitions, disappointment, disasters and losses?

A full, mature relationship between a parent and a child and between parent and parent requires the freedom to be spontaneous, open and give expression to all feelings and needs. When a parent finds difficulty with either the expression of or the receptivity to certain feelings and events, it is important for her own as well as the family's development to seek the reasons and find the support and means to resolve these serious emotional, social and behavioural blocks. It is also incumbent on the other parent or other adult who witnesses these restrictive practices to confront positively and firmly the mother who is blocked. Confrontation is an act of love and belief that the person who is vulnerable has the need and the capacity to free herself from her emotional imprisonment.

It is my experience and belief that no parent ever wants to deliberately block their children's progress, or indeed their own. However, for those parents who cannot be upset, considerable support is required for them to touch into and express their unlimited power to cope with the stresses and upsets of life. Any hint of criticism or judgement convinces them of how unsafe the world is and, rightly, they will retreat into their 'don't upset me' mode.

## Q5. WHAT HAPPENS WHEN A PARENT LIVES HIS OR HER LIFE THROUGH THE CHILD?

Democratic family living is based on love and mutual respect. If only one person in a relationship is granted respect, there is no equality; this is as true for an adult-child relationship as it is for an adult-adult relationship. Parents and teachers need to ensure that they demonstrate respect for the child and her rights. This demands sensitivity in achieving a balance between expecting too little and expecting too much. It also entails asking the question: whose life is the child living, her own or yours? Take, for example, the following case:

Mary, aged fifteen years, is one of two children of high achieving parents, both at the pinnacle of their respective professions. Mary had cleverly learned to conform to her parents' high expectations of themselves and of her. Both parents have extremely high standards for behaviour and academic development. Excellence in all fields of endeavour is expected – schoolwork, athletics, piano, dress, manners and tidiness. Any grade less than A is viewed with strong disapproval. Everyone comments on how intelligent and extraordinary Mary is and how lucky the parents are to have such a 'brilliant' child. However, Mary exhibits certain physical symptoms that the parents are currently worried about, but choose to do nothing about; she complains of abdominal pains, has a nervous twitch in her neck, has nightmares and walks in her sleep.

Mary's parents are subconsciously neglectful in their 'great expectations'. Since Mary intuitively knows the importance of success to her parents and the dangers of 'failure' to them and to her, she pleases her parents by living up to their unrealistic expectations. But she reveals clear signs of inner turmoil. She knows too well that she only has significance as long as she pleases her parents and is on top. She does not dare to lose her top position by rebelling overtly against their demands. She can only indirectly express her protest through her body and in her sleep.

Mary's parents show a deep disrespect for her as a person; they use her merely as a means of enhancing their own prestige. Mary cannot respect herself or live her own life when her whole life is geared towards meeting her parents' needs for her achievements. Unless the parents see, face and free themselves of their addiction to success, it is unlikely that Mary will find the emotional safety to express how oppressed she feels and her need to discover and live her own unique life.

As I have already mentioned, the sad reality is that parents can only bring their children to the same level of maturity they have reached themselves. No doubt, the source of the parents' identifying their worth with work achievements lies in their own family of origin. In working with families I have found that I can trace the origins of the presenting difficulties back at least five generations. There is no suggestion here that Mary's parents are being deliberately cruel. Indeed, they are as neglectful of themselves (driven by their overwhelming need to succeed) as they are of their daughter's emotional and social progress. However, as adults we have a responsibility to sort out our own emotional baggage, so that we do not block the progress of others.

Given the high rise in demand for individual, couple and family counselling, there is no doubt that people are attempting to understand and resolve their emotional baggage. However, it is sometimes the case that a parent brings a reluctant partner, child or adolescent for help, but does not see herself as having any problems. When the counsellor begins to probe the influence of that parent on the marriage or the children's lives, no further appointments are sought.

The child who is considered 'brilliant' in the family is rarely seen as being more psychologically at risk than the child who struggles academically. More often than not it is the latter child who is perceived as having a problem and is often brought to a range of experts to 'diagnose' the problem. The reality is that both children are in need of help and the therapy of choice needs to be family focused. However, the child who attempts to achieve the ambitions of her parents is more at risk because of the constant pressure she is under and her intense fear of failure.

Another aspect to the story about Mary above is that she has a brother who hates school, refuses to do his homework and causes considerable disruption in school and at home. The boy's subconscious strategy is to reduce his parents' expectations by 'playing the fool' and being aggressive. Whereas Mary had never been brought to any expert before, Mark had seen several medical, psychological and educational professionals. Profound change is needed within and between the parents for Mark to regain his motivation to learn and for Mary to live her own life and embrace life as an adventure rather than a constant test.

## Q6. I'M ASHAMED TO SAY THAT I FREQUENTLY FEEL DISAPPOINTED WITH MY HUSBAND AND CHILDREN AND I DON'T KNOW WHAT TO DO ABOUT IT. CAN YOU HELP?

Disappointment is an emotional and psychological experience and can have the same telling effects of such powerful emotions as love, hate, fear, sadness, grief, anger and jealousy. The expression of 'I'm disappointed in you', accompanied by all its non-verbal partners of expressionless face, stiff lips, steely eyes and erect body posture, can be a devastating blow and a clear message that you have not lived up to expectations.

You can experience disappointment in three ways: the first is where you feel disappointed in another, the second, in yourself and the third, when another expresses disappointment in you.

Generally speaking, when you feel disappointment in a relationship, important needs – expressed or unexpressed – have not been met and your feelings of disappointment give testament to 'being let down'. This can occur in all relationships – between husband and wife, lover and lover, friend and friend, employer and employee, parent and child and teacher and child. A common cry in marital conflict is 'I'm disappointed in my marriage'. This statement speaks a thousand words about unfulfilled expectations, loss of love and anger, and it often signals the beginnings of the break-up of the relationship. When parents say to a son or daughter 'You're a disappointment to us', they are expressing their anger at their child for not turning out the way they wanted. The disappointment may be around their son's or daughter's choice of friend, university course or career; it may also have to do with some behaviour that in their eyes has brought shame on the family – teenage pregnancy, taking drugs, being drunk, stealing, lying and so on. However, true love and effective parenting is born from under-standing, and the judgement and condemnation in 'I'm disappointed in you' shows no glimmer of such maturity. You might say to me 'But I am feeling disappointed and what are you going to do about that?' All feelings, including disap-pointment, are messages to the person experiencing them and are looking to you to own, interpret and take the responsible action prompted by the feelings. When disap-pointment has arisen from unmet needs, then detecting and taking responsibility for those needs are what is required. It is not your partner's, or friend's, or employer's, or child's responsibility to meet your needs – that is your task. You have every right to make requests around unmet needs, but it may often be the case that the other person is not in a place to respond to those needs. Understanding the latter makes it more likely that the significant other may make greater efforts to meet your needs once they are reasonable. Some feelings of disappointment arise when the other person is not living their life according to your wishes, but then each person is here to live their own life, and respect and cherishing of that freedom make for far less disappoint-ment in another. Certainly, when your reasonable needs continue to be unmet, then action on your part will be required. For example, in an unhappy relationship, you state: 'I have talked to you about my unfulfilled needs and I see that you are not in a place to respond. I intend now to create new friendships so that I'm not lonely when you continue to work all the time.'

The expression 'I'm disappointed in you' can vary in depth and intensity, depending on which word accompanies 'disappointed', for example 'terribly disappointed' or 'very disappointed'. Probably the expression 'bitter disappointment' conveys most powerfully the intense hurt and anger experienced when entirely reasonable expectations have not been met. However, no matter how reasonable your expectations are, meeting them, ultimately, lies at your door.

When you feel disappointed in yourself, that in some way you have let yourself down, the feeling signals a need for you to reflect on some aspect of your behaviour. When such reflection does not follow the feeling of disappointment, the risk of depression is high. The more intense feeling of depression is a louder cry for reflection. Disappointment in self may be due to going against strong values, and this signals either the questioning of these values or working to reinforce their practice. Disappointment in self may also arise when you have 'worn your heart on your sleeve', looking for another to take care of you or show interest in you. Here reflection will invite you to deepen your relationship with self and to express directly and clearly your needs.

When another expresses disappointment in you, it is important to listen and to understand that the expression 'I'm so disappointed in you' is not a criticism of you, but an attempt by the person to express some unmet need. If you react, conflict will ensue; if you proact, then resolution is possible. A reaction could take the form of 'I'm sick of your complaining'; a proaction would gently enquire 'tell me more about what you are feeling disappointed about?' It is essential that the receiver, rather than becoming the rescuer, becomes the enabler so that the person expressing disappointment can come into ownership of his or her own feelings, unmet needs and the required action to meet those needs.

## Q7. MY HUSBAND HAS A SERIOUS DRINK PROBLEM BUT TOTALLY DENIES IT AND HOW IT AFFECTS ME AND THE CHILDREN. WHAT SHOULD I DO?

As the Corkman rightly said 'denial is not a river in Egypt' but a very powerful protection that a child or adult employs under severe threat.

There are two kinds of denial, both of which serve a similar purpose. The first type of denial is more common in childhood and involves repression of some major violation of the child's physical, sexual or emotional wellbeing. The second kind is common to adults and involves the amazing capacity to compartmentalise difficult aspects of life or neglectful actions towards self or others and not allow them in any way to inform your daily life.

In repression, the child blocks out from her consciousness any memory of the horrific violation. This 'locked away' trauma may never resurface unless some event in later life forcefully mirrors the dark events of the past and there is present in the person's life some person(s) who is emotionally safe, non-judgemental, compassionate and unconditionally loving. It is not surprising that in the practice of psychotherapy a client may suddenly begin to recall the buried horror. This lifting of repression is a total experience, an actual reliving of the traumatic experiences, and is both terrifying and freeing for the person.

Repression is not a weakness but an astounding intuitive and intelligent act in which the person engages to safeguard her sacred self from further desecration. There are psychologists who believe that denial is a way of blocking out feelings of weakness and helplessness in the face of overwhelming neglect. However, my own belief is that human behaviour always makes sense, is always powerful and that the purpose of denial is to block off the expression of power. The child who has been violated knows unconsciously that she would be in even greater danger if she expressed her power by breaking the silence and naming the perpetrator. The child who represses knows that, in the words of Nelson Mandela, 'our deepest fear is that we are powerful beyond measure'. All throughout the person's life the spirit will look for opportunities to release the repressed events and may manifest powerful physical symptoms in the hope that the strong understanding, emotional safety and support that is required will be offered by some health practitioner. Sometimes a victim's support group can be the catalyst to the lifting of repression.

But you might well ask where is the power in the denial of one's own vulnerabilities, unhappy relationships or the death of a child or the denial of a serious illness by a loved one. For example, some individuals with a serious alcohol addiction or serious anorexic condition or who have been given a diagnosis of terminal cancer will deny that there is anything wrong with them. It is important that others realise that this is an unconscious defense mechanism and that the person is utterly convinced of what they are saying. Indeed, the more another person tries to make them 'bite the bullet' of the reality of their pyschosomatic condition, the more they become entrenched in their denial.

The issue regarding alcoholism and anorexia nervosa is that these conditions are an attempt to fill the void within ('full to the brim with alcohol') or to keep at bay any further 'invasions' (physical or sexual or emotional). Ask yourself how do you treat a person with anorexia nervosa? With kid gloves! As long as any illness or addiction protects the self from further abuse and blocks off the expression of power ('bottled up' in alcoholism and 'starved of' in anorexia), the person will maintain denial of these conditions. However, unconsciously they have no wish to stay in the protected places, and when the caring they receive is empathic, congruent, non-judgemental and unconditionally loving, they will slowly but surely bring forward the hidden reasons for their addictive behaviours. It is not what individuals show in terms of problematic behaviours that needs to be changed, but rather what they don't show needs to be the focus of attention.

The denial of serious illness in a loved one tends to be more short-lived. Again the loved one's serious illness may be a manifestation of unexpressed deeper emotional conflicts and the tremendous support received around the illness can create the emotional safety long craved. This can lead to an acceptance of (and sometimes a recovery from) the illness. The denial of the death of a child or partner can be related to an emotional dying experienced in childhood which is now reappearing for healing purposes. Do not get me wrong, the death of a loved one is always a hugely painful experience, one that we all have to face several times in our lives. Such grief is conscious. Denial is unconscious and though it involves the deep loss of a loved one, at the hidden level it certainly involves some great unresolved loss within oneself that dared not be expressed, perhaps up to this point in time.

Compassion is essential to our responding to individuals who are in denial; judgement and criticism will only deepen the unconscious protective process. However, those who are at the receiving end of the neglectful actions of a person in denial or who are daily witnessing the emaciation of a person who is starving herself need to get help and support for themselves. The unconscious denial behaviours of one person cannot be allowed to become a neglect of another, but too often this is the case.

## Q8. AS A PARENT I SUFFER FROM DEPRESSION. HOW CAN I BEST OVERCOME THIS?

I met a young woman recently who, since she was sixteen years of age, has been in and out of both private and public psychiatric hospitals. She is now twenty-one years of age. She has made several suicide attempts and periodically becomes obsessed with doing away with herself. Psychiatrists have told her there is no obvious precipitant for her depression – such as sexual abuse, physical violence, parents' separation – and that therefore she has a biological depression. The advice is that she stays on anti-depressant medication for the rest of her life. Ironically, the medication appears to have done little for her over the years. Suicide ideation and despair continue. Isolation from parents, siblings and peers is persisting. She also feels unable to leave home to go to college or work. Furthermore, the hopeless biological diagnosis and prognosis has in turn left her feeling hopeless and she declares 'what's the point in living if I have this incurable depression? How can I hold down a job, enjoy a relationship, get married, have a family, take on a mortgage with this interminable millstone around my neck?'

One of the positives that the psychiatrist pointed out to her parents is that 'she loves to listen to music'. What is sadly fascinating is that the major reason for her depression can be detected in the lyrics of the music she constantly plays. But because of the biological mindset there is no expansive listening to this young woman's experiences. The song she most likes to listen to has the line 'I wish I was special, but I'm a creep', which projects very clearly her strong sense of worthlessness and invisibility.

There is nothing darker than not having a sense of your own value, sacredness, uniqueness and vast potential to understand the world you live in.

Both of this young woman's parents have grave self-worth difficulties and neither were in a position to inspire their daughter with an acceptance and celebration of herself. Whilst there would have been no one major neglectful experience – like sexual abuse or violence – there was the everyday experience of invisibility due to lack of contact by one parent and unrealistic expectations by the other. It is not only adults who experience lives of 'quiet desperation'.

My own clinical experience of people who present with depression is that there are always psycho-social reasons for their condition and that a holistic exploration with them of their unique biographical histories inevitably reveals patterns of relationships that explain the depression.

Getting to the causes does not lift the depression, but the breaking of the silence and the witnessing by me of the blocking experiences to the real expression of self are important stepping stones. What is vital is the presence of a strong connection between the psychologist and the young person, so that the young person knows and feels that there is one person who is there for her. The involvement of parents is crucial and my own experience is that the majority of parents more than willingly cooperate in their offspring's discovery of self and her or his need to be loved and accepted by them. Indeed, very often the young person's crisis is the catalyst for the parents to own and take responsibility for their own darkened sense of self and the troubled relationships between each other and their children.

There is no intention here to blame parents or other significant adults for the lives of those who are depressed. Parents, teachers, relatives and siblings always do their best within the confines of their own vulnerabilities. You can only bring children to the same level of development you have reached yourself. Nevertheless, though parents or others are not responsible *for* their offspring's depression, they are responsible *to* the behaviour they have perpetrated that, albeit unwittingly, has darkened the presence of their son or daughter.

This is a difficult task – for parents or others to face the shadow inside themselves and own the fact that their own darkness begets darkness in their children. The light of honesty, openness, expression of regret, declaration of unconditional love and the presence of understanding, support, patience, compassion and encouragement can go a long way to helping their unhappy offspring emerge from the shadows of depression.

## Q9. I KNOW I AM SUCH A PERFECTIONIST, BUT I FIND IT SO HARD TO LET GO OF HAVING TO DO EVERY-THING RIGHT. WHAT DO I NEED TO DO?

It is not easy to work, live and play with individuals who are perfectionistic.

They constantly drive both themselves and others, especially at times of added stress. They are critical and intolerant of others who do not work to their specific standards, as this in their minds would reflect their own failure. Unfortunately, such success achieved at the cost of pain to others rarely brings inner peace.

At home, perfectionists can become irritable and aggressive, appearing insensitive to the needs and feelings of those who surround them. One man described this situation well when he told me 'how the house looks and having everything in its right place are more important to my wife than how myself and the children feel'. Furthermore, when confronted, perfectionists may attack or adopt a defensive role, crying or withdrawing from company. However, no change occurs in their extreme behaviour.

Perfectionists fear failure and compete to reach a goal which they believe will give them security. Sadly, the goal posts keep shifting as high achievements mean having to maintain such performance in order not to fall from grace. They strive to keep achieving, for this is a measure of their success, and success is a measure of their worth as a person.

Not only are perfectionists competitive in their work, but they equally are so in their leisure interests, whatever the activity. They can become easily paranoid if they feel that their superior position is threatened by another person, and, indeed, may drop out of the race.

Perfectionists find it difficult to rest for fear that they might miss an opportunity on the ladder to success; they are always busy 'doing something'. Even when they are sitting, they fidget and their minds are overactive. There is never enough time and they are intolerant of queues and waiting. They would rather go without than wait.

They live in the past or in the future, missing out on the pleasure of the present. You can recognise them by their body language: when walking the head is forward already at work planning the day ahead; their legs and bottom are dragging behind in the past, still attached to the happenings of the morning before they left home.

Perfectionists have a desperate need to be in control and may be fastidious with their belongings – straightening pictures, indexing records and becoming agitated when someone replaces a book on the shelf in the wrong order.

They work by the rules, placing people and objects in pigeon-holes. Here they are safe; they know where they stand and can feel secure. However, their security is easily threatened. For example, if anything or anybody disturbs their carefully controlled environment they become irritable and anxious. They do not cope well with change and yet their search for perfection places them in an ever-changing environment. The result is a constant need to place a finger on the stress button so that they are always alert to the perils of the world.

Inevitably, the hidden insecurities of perfectionism reveal themselves in diseases in the body. These include panic attacks with palpitations, hyperventilation, frequency of passing urine and bowel movements and muscle spasm. The physical body is out of control and reflects the emotional out-of-control position of the perfectionist.

Commonly, these physical symptoms appear at times of rest, especially in the middle of the night. The perfectionist will complain that 'I cannot understand this; when I rest the symptoms appear'. I explain that while they are busy, their conscious mind manages to control the activities of the body. During rest or sleep, when the conscious mind switches off, this control is released and the subconscious is allowed to reveal the hidden insecurities through the physical symptoms.

All of these symptoms provide the individual with the opportunity to rest and to review their life. However, rather than seizing the opportunity for change, perfectionists see the physical symptoms as aggravations and a disruption to their busy life, leading to frustration and anger. The message of the disease is lost. Sadly, it may take a more serious illness for the message to be seen.

Perfectionists often have been reared in a family where success was valued and love was attached to success. It is a classic case of conditional love: 'Be successful and I will love you.' The resultant emotional driving force is 'be perfect', and unless this condition is released it is carried throughout adult life.

To feel real and solid security, the perfectionist needs to realise his worth, value, uniqueness, sacredness and gifted-ness. He needs to know that nothing adds to or takes away from his sacred person. He needs to experience living, working and playing as explorations of the world, but not as measures of his worth. Through this gradual realisation the perfectionist will experience inner peace, confidence and peace with others and the world.

## Q10. I FEEL SO ASHAMED OF MYSELF WHEN I CRY. WHAT CAN I DO TO ENSURE THAT I DON'T PASS THIS SHAME ON TO MY CHILDREN?

What is it that causes people to feel ashamed around certain actions and feelings? When a woman cries, she will avert her head and not make any eye contact, and when asked about it she will say, 'I feel ashamed at making such a fool of myself'. Men experience even more powerful feelings of shame when tears come to their eyes; they choke back the tears and leave the scene before anybody spots their vulnerable state. Shame also arises around feelings of depression, helplessness, anxiety, jealousy and envy. All of these feelings are important emotional barometers and signal the need for some changes within or without or in both directions. Unfortunately, when shame arises it acts as a block to expression of those feelings, and so the opportunities for mature progress go abegging.

Infants and toddlers spontaneously express a whole range of feelings and actions. It is not the child's actions or feelings that generate shame, but the responses of adults to their display. When adults are not comfortable with certain feelings or have taboos around sexual expression or spontaneous expression of achievements, they will tend to demonstrate disapproval when children exhibit such behaviour. For example, the little girl who uninhibitedly does somersaults may be stopped in her tracks by her mother who is uncomfortable about her child's panties showing. The child's free expression is not only halted but, intuitively, the child senses her mother's disapproval and this becomes a risk to her mother's acceptance of her. Children know that they cannot survive without their parents and they conform to the restrictions imposed by parents in order to offset threats to their welfare. Unconsciously and cleverly, the feeling of shame arises around the taboo feeling or action and will persist into adulthood. However, if the adult person does not reflect on what causes them to feel shame in certain situations it is likely they will carry that shame to the grave with them. It also means that if they have children the cycle of shame will be repeated.

Along with disapproval, showing scorn or ridicule and physical punishment all play their part in generating shame. When a child demonstrates an interest in something that the adult feels uncomfortable with or feels is inappropriate, the child's interest becomes buried and the feelings of shame arise to protect him from further excursions into that taboo area of behaviour. Ironically, it is the adult who needs to reflect on their punishing responses to the child's behaviour; in so doing they have the opportunity to free themselves of shame and release feelings and behaviours that went underground when they were children.

In the most benign ways children can experience condemnation of their experiences. The little boy who cries when his mother is leaving him with the playschool teacher is told there is no need to get upset because Mammy will be back soon. This well-intentioned comment is designed to comfort the child, but in reality it has the effect of diluting what the child is feeling and it invalidates the child's feeling of being upset. Not only does the child feel misunderstood, but he also feels embarrassed for being upset in the first place. Later on, when as an adult he feels upset when his girlfriend is away, he will be fearful of telling her or others what he is feeling as his expectation is that he will be ridiculed for displaying such 'weakness'. The shame he experiences will now limit his ability to be intimate and his girlfriend may believe that 'he doesn't miss me when I'm not around'. Not only will he cover up his 'shameful' feelings but he may have the further defence of appearing nonchalant and uncaring (the exact opposite of what he really feels). No wonder so many relationships become confusing and troubled. When relationships operate at the level of defences it is inevitable that conflict will emerge. The purpose of conflict is a creative opportunity for each of the parties to the relationship to wake up to their respective imprisoned states and to set about freeing themselves of shame.

When a person demonstrates shame around an action or a feeling, it helps enormously when the other person maintains an unjudging gaze and a compassionate listening. Such emotional support means that the person does not have to feel ashamed about having such feelings in the first place. With the 'shame' block removed she can now give full vent to her internal state.

# CHAPTER SIX

# HOW CAN PARENTS PREPARE CHILDREN FOR LIVING THEIR LIVES FULLY?

## INTRODUCTION

How many parents can honestly say they love failure and see success as having the same purpose as failure – to set the next learning challenge? How many parents can assert that school tests and state examinations are mere (and crude) measures of knowledge and no index of the intelligence of their child or themselves? Indeed, children as young as five and six years of age complain of being all stressed out by school tests. Children quickly pick up on parents' and teachers' fears of failure, their addiction to success and the threat to self that examinations pose. When parents are in touch with their own vast intellectual potential, they readily recognise and affirm the genius that each child is. The confusion of knowledge with intelligence has led to unfortunate intellectual labelling of children, thereby posing a great block to their realisation of their intellectual potential.

Parents are the primary educators of children and unless parents free themselves of their fears around learning and work and their doubts about their own intelligence, they cannot be a source of inspiration for their children. The pursuit of knowledge and the development of life and work skills need to be seen by children as an adventure, an exciting and wonderful challenge. Toddlers exhibit a love of and eagerness to learn, an adventuresomeness and a fearlessness. The pity is that they encounter parents and teachers who have had to hide these admirable qualities and they take on the fears of their parents and teachers or else emotionally and intellectually perish.

Parents wish so much for their children, but their good intentions are so often shattered by their own dependencies on success, of what other people say and the almost universal fear of failure.

As with every other behaviour, parents need to look to their own responses before they are in a mature position to foster desirable qualities in their children. A crucial issue here is to ensure that a child's academic progress is not confused with his unique self. Each child aspires to different areas of knowledge and also develops a unique learning style. Appreciation of this fact by parents can reduce a lot of heartache for children who do not appear to 'fit in' to the school system. Seeing and affirming how each child uniquely and determinedly expresses his individuality in selecting knowledge areas that set him apart from the other children in the family is the foundation to ensuring that learning remains an adventure.

Parents, too, need to champion children whose presence and love of learning are jeopardised by either the other parent, by a sibling or, indeed, by a teacher. Championing children is about ensuring that they are exposed to positive learning environments, wherein all learning occurs in an atmosphere of mutual respect and caring between parent and child, teacher and child, and child and child. Bullying is an important threat for parents to detect and corrective action needs to include empowering children to stand up for themselves. Parents need to give their child every support to do so.

Peer pressure can also result in children abandoning their ambitions or diluting their eagerness to learn in order to fit in with the expectations of their peer group. Talking *with* (not *at* or *to*) children on such sudden changes in learning patterns can help to resolve the situation. It is unwise for parents to believe it is transient and hope that time will heal whatever has caused the learning block. No matter what the challenge, ultimately it is action that brings about the mature responses needed.

Patience, encouragement, humour and supporting the child 'to do it himself' are essential qualities for parents to show when they are helping a child with school homework or teaching a child any activity. Impatience, criticism, comparisons, put-downs, sarcasm, crossness, labelling and pushing or hitting are just some of the experiences that either drive children to hate and avoid learning or to strive to always get it right. There are children as young as six or seven who will not take on a new challenge when there is a possibility they might not be the best. The difference between a child who loves to learn and a child who is perfectionistic is that the former is motivated by an intrinsic love of learning and the latter by a fear of failure and dependence on success. Another difference is that children who have maintained the adventure of learning are expansive in their interests, whilst those children who are perfectionists are restricted to the areas of knowledge, work or sport in which they demonstrate high performance.

Younger children learn much through participating in adult activities. Children love to help their mums and dads but they are also quite adamant about 'wanting to do it myself'. 'Response-ableness', which is the *sine qua non* to responsibility, emerges by allowing children to 'just do it'. Parents need to accept the initial mess because all learning starts in that way. Parents who are perfectionistic, short-tempered and fussy can experience difficulty in holding back on their anger or resisting the urge to do it for the child. Both of these responses deprive children of the practice opportunities they require in order to become 'response-able'. Furthermore, when parents cannot put up with the mess in the early days of a child's life, they will face a far greater mess later on when their adolescent son or daughter refuses to study, drops out of school and has little ambition.

Feedback to children on their learning progress needs to be done in a way that nurtures learning efforts. To feed is to nurture, and encouraging and praising learning efforts and seeing that for every learning effort there is always an attainment are essential acts of nurturing children's education. The most significant attainment is that the child has made the effort, and this deserves recognition. Even a misspelt word often has some letters of the word properly placed and even when all the letters are incorrect, the child has formed other letters. The emphasis on performance, on getting it right, has dried up in many children the flow of their intrinsic love of learning. It is far safer not to make the effort, or do the minimum, or strain to get it right so that humiliation is eliminated – how clever!

## Q1. HOW ARE LANGUAGE SKILLS BEST DEVELOPED IN CHILDREN?

There was a time in Ireland when the language development of children was seriously disrupted by what was known as 'linguistic chaos'. The phenomenon of 'linguistic chaos' was peculiar to large families, where the many children and parents all tended to speak at once, making it very difficult to listen, learn and become articulate.

Children best learn their language through one-to-one contact with a parent or guardian. The combination of action with words speeds up language development. Many mothers, when engaging in a domestic activity, or including the child in the activity, tend to verbally bring the child step-by-step through the activity.

It would appear that the 'linguistic chaos' of large families and the 'linguistic sophistication' of smaller families are being replaced by a new phenomenon, which is posing a serious block to language development in both types of families. Alan Wells, the director of the Basic Skills Agency, which is the English and Welsh National Development Organisation for literacy and numeracy, claims that 'a succession of grunts and gestures is replacing conversation between children and their parents in more and more homes'.

It would appear that children are increasingly spending their leisure time staring at computer screens while surfing the internet or mesmerised by television programmes or playing hi-tech play-station games. Many parents have also become computer or television addicted. The results are that family meals are becoming a thing of the past, leaving few opportunities between family members for mature conversation. There is evidence that indicates that many children starting school possess very few language skills. This clearly has an impact on children's learning as they go through the early stages of school. It would seem, too, that poor language development is affecting children from both working class and affluent families. Affluent families have the added situation of career parents working long hours, leading to limited communication.

Remedies for children's deteriorating grasp of language include ensuring that childminders engage in one-to-one conversation with children or that parents attend classes that teach them how to converse and play in meaningful ways with their children. Certainly, instant aids would be to reinstate family mealtimes, remove the television and computer from the dining area and ban the playing of computer games during mealtimes. Also, one or two days weekly of no television or computer provide opportunities for family conversation. Consistency and firmness in these issues are required by parents, not only to enhance language development, but, even more importantly, to create opportunities for all family members to make real contact with each other at certain points of the day. Furthermore, it is the height of disrespect to the person who has prepared the meal and to other family members to engage in television watching or computer playing or newspaper reading during mealtimes. However, parents need to lead through their own considerate behaviour and not have double standards, i.e. they need to model 'do as I do' rather than 'do as I say'. Parents need to stoutly resist a child's or adolescent's insistence that he or she carries their meal into the television or computer area. They should not be put off if the new family arrangements are met with initial indifference or 'what's to talk about' responses.

I have long been an advocate of weekly family meetings to discuss the running of the family, the needs of each family member and the allocation of responsibilities, as well as the airing of difficulties and grievances that inevitably arise in all families. Such meetings, where each family member is encouraged and supported to speak for himself or herself would, undoubtedly, improve linguistic skills. These meetings would certainly add to family harmony. Children also love stories, particularly about their parents' childhood, and these verbal excursions are a great source of language development. Reading to younger children and sharing and discussing books with older children also helps.

As with all things, balance is what matters, and it is important to prioritise opportunities for loving contact between family members. Sitting in front of the television or computer is fine once families eat together and talk to each other, making sure that each person is given the chance to talk and that the others actively listen at any one time. Grunts and verbally unaccompanied gestures are not respectful means of communication, and these quickly disappear when no response is shown to their display. You can be sure when children or adults do not get what they want through grunts and gestures, they speedily learn to respectfully articulate their needs.

## Q2. HOW CAN I ENSURE MY CHILD HAS A SATISFYING CAREER?

The place for parents on the playing field of young people's career decision-making is on the sidelines, ready to offer support, encouragement and financial resources. It is not wise for parents to project their own ambitions onto their offspring. Children are here to live their own lives and not the lives of their parents. However, it was not too long ago that going into the priesthood was seen as a highly desirable career, even more so than teaching, medicine and nursing, and there was the common belief that it was the mother who had the vocation, and not the young man! Have things changed?

In recent years I have helped young people who were afraid, sometimes terrified, to tell their parents that the profession they were pursuing was not what they really wanted to do. Parents who are into prestige rather than the unique person of each family member often subconsciously put pressure on their children to follow in their father's or mother's footsteps. Signs of this are that in some of the socially approved professions of medicine, education, law and high finance, there are often two or three generations of the same family. Bitter disappointment, even emotional rejection, can occur when a son or daughter does not conform to the expectations of parents.

Certainly, there may be a serious motivation issue when young people choose to go on a particular third-level course for one or more of the following reasons:

- 'anything to get out of home'
- 'to please my parents'

- □ 'to be with my friends'
- □ 'to please my teachers'
- □ to enjoy the craic'
- □ 'because the college plays rugby'

Parents may be throwing good money after bad when they finance any of the above reasons. Some possible outcomes are that the young person will drop out, do little or no study, or show over-the-top dedication or become 'a perpetual student'. Parents may feel fortunate when their son is highly committed, but burnout and sickness may result in an effort to escape being in a career not chosen by oneself.

The key to choosing a career is to pursue what is important to you. Young people are not born knowing what their core needs and drives are. It helps to ask questions about what types of experiences brought you fulfilment in the past? What inspired you? What did you have (and maybe still have) a passion for doing? What activity motivated you to get up each day? What activities truly excited and moved you?

All people have certain experiences they crave in order to feel satisfaction and fulfilment in life: experiences like belonging, acceptance, understanding, achievement, adventure, spiritual meaning. While these needs vary from person to person, each person's sense of quality of life is directly related to how well these needs are met. These core fulfilment needs are central to a career choice and need to be met in college, in the workplace, and in all areas of a person's life, or self-esteem starts to suffer.

When a young person lacks sureness and self-confidence and is bedevilled by all sorts of doubts, fears and insecurities, making a career choice is not a priority issue. Indeed, taking a year out to do some self-work is more important than launching oneself on a career path. Self-work is the most important work of all and it is the bedrock for all explorations: relationships, work, interests, spirituality, sports, travel and so on.

A common happening nowadays is young people taking a year out to travel, mostly down under in Australia and New Zealand. I am all for such an adventure before pursuing a career, but I sometimes wonder would the young people benefit more from an inner down under journey to discover the wonder, power, uniqueness and sacredness of the self that lies within? Certainly, my experience is that not long after coming home from their travels, many of the insecurities they had before they left rapidly re-emerge. An outer journey does not necessarily lead to a lessening of insecurity and a deepening of maturity.

Most of all, I would encourage young people to be true to themselves, as the lies that deeply affect our self-esteem are not so much the lies we tell as the lies we live. Be sure, too, that your chosen life path has a heart. If it doesn't, it is of no use; if it does, the path is good.

## Q3. ISN'T SUCCESS THE MOST IMPORTANT EXPERIENCE MY CHILD REQUIRES FOR A HAPPY LIFE?

In the pluralist society and economic prosperity of the 'new' Ireland, not only are parents expected to be up-to-date in designer fashion and new cars, they are expected to have dynamic and well-paid jobs, be available at all times on their mobile phones for work and family concerns, be sexually active and 'with it', be in touch with their feelings and the feelings and concerns of their children, have high self-esteem, provide for their children's education (often up to the age of twenty-five years) and be on hand for their children.

Quite a tall order for a parent who may work a daily minimum of eight hours outside the home and as many hours inside the home. Mothers still carry 90 per cent of domestic and parenting responsibilities. Fathers or partners are often working twelve-hour days, and that does not include commuting time. It is getting increasingly difficult to get experienced and trained childminders, so that the working parent frequently has to deal with the fall-out from the emotional under-involvement and limited parenting skills of some childminders.

Another product of the 'success' culture is that some parents resort to bribing their children with expensive holidays or designer outfits or money for high academic performance, sometimes as early as primary-school years. Such behaviour stems from parents' own subconscious addiction to success. These parents would do well to listen to Bill Gates, who says, 'the greatest impediment to progress is success'.

While I thoroughly agree with his concept, I suspect his billionaire status will have some people cast a cynical eye on the wisdom of his observation. It reminds me of the young woman who had a profound spiritual experience during a retreat, and on my enquiry about whether she would now give more time to spirituality, she replied: 'I don't think I've had enough materialism yet.'

It is difficult for people to resist the overwhelming tide of materialism that is present, but there is a danger that 'having will become the sinister enemy of being'.

The cornerstone of effective parenting is being in touch with your own sacred self, uniqueness, individuality, vast capability and inherent goodness. This can only be experienced fully in the stillness of 'not doing', in the power of emptiness, where you touch into your real worth, which is separate from what you do.

Equally, being there in a similar way for partner and children is central to effective, enduring and fulfilling relationships. There is nothing more powerful than the love that is communicated in the silent embrace of another.

There is no doubt that many parents are concerned about the new, different and materialistic pace of Irish life. They are acutely aware of having less time to listen to and talk to children; they are worried about teenage sex, teenage pregnancies and the ever-increasing academic competitiveness children are facing.

Parents have anxieties too regarding getting the best education and career prospects for their offspring. Furthermore, they are rightly concerned about the effects of the rising level of marital and family breakdown on children. These concerns are worthy of attention and, in all aspects of parenting, parents firstly need to address themselves.

I do not want to be a success spoilsport. On the contrary, we deserve to celebrate the fruits of our labours and our emergence from an oppressive political and religious history, where we protected ourselves by being inferior. There is now a real surge of power in the Celtic psyche where the Irish in the world are seen as models for business acumen, drive, ambition, political and social progress. Our achievements in the arenas of music, sport and literature are widely acknowledged.

However, we must guard against swinging into superiority and know that the power we are discovering in ourselves is in everyone. We must also keep in our sights that love is vital for human life and that a successful economic and progressive culture that loses sight of that fundamental value will eventually collapse in on itself. In homes, schools, workplaces, communities and churches, the celebration, respect and valuing of the sacredness of each human being must not be swallowed up by the wave of success.

Parents and leaders, in particular, need to model a lifestyle that is balanced and which places priority on the care and love of self and others. They also need to demonstrate an expansiveness of life, keep a good sense of humour and show that life is an adventure and not a trial.

## Q4. HOW CAN I HELP MY CHILD RETAIN HER LOVE OF LEARNING?

All learning needs to be an adventure, an excitement, a challenge to the minds, hearts and spirits of those in pursuit of excellence. Furthermore, education needs to focus not only on preparing people intellectually and occupationally for life, but also on developing their social, emotional, sexual, political and spiritual potential. When there is imbalance in the holistic development of individuals, it seriously blocks overall effectiveness. For example, the high-achieving academic, who has no clue how to develop and maintain emotional closeness with others, is a serious risk to himself and to those with whom he interacts.

This imbalance in education is also evident in the training of teachers, where undue emphasis is put on 'what to teach' but little emphasis on the 'how' of teaching. Furthermore, teachers carry into the classroom considerable emotional baggage from their own histories of education in homes and schools, and, unless their complexes, dependencies and fears around education are resolved, they will pass on this baggage. No opportunities exist either during or after training for teachers to reflect on and resolve these deep-seated difficulties. There is the added problem that many teachers have lost their motivation to teach, because many of their needs go unheeded by governments and unions, and they are in no fit place to inspire children to retain their love of learning.

Parents are the primary educators, and by the time some children come to school they have already lost their love and eagerness to learn. Evidence of such loss is lack of motivation, poor or little concentration, rebelliousness, hyperactivity, sickness, timidity, fearfulness and perfectionism. Whereas preparation for teaching is largely inadequate and requires radical rethinking, there is absolutely no preparation for parenting. The first three years of a child's life are crucial to his or her future, and the training of parents for the complex task of rearing and educating children is a challenge that successive governments fail to take on. Like teachers, parents subconsciously project their problems onto children.

It is a well-established fact that leaders in any field of endeavour (for example, parenting, teaching, therapy, politics, medicine) can only bring their charges to the same level of development they have reached themselves.

The future of society does not lie with children, but with adults. When I help children and adolescents who are deeply distressed, I can sometimes trace back the origins of their problems five generations. This phenomenon has nothing to do with genetics, but all to do with adults not taking on the responsibilities to resolve their own emotional, social, educational, sexual and spiritual difficulties. It is also the responsibility of political and social agencies to provide the opportunities for adults to get the help and support needed to pursue liberation from their fears. Only when adults are liberated will their presence liberate children.

One of the great tragedies of education today is how what was once intrinsically driven has become extrinsically driven.

Intrinsic to learning are the rotating experiences of failure and success; these are the gems of learning. However, the practice of employing failure as a stick with which to beat children and adults, and success as a carrot to motivate, has effectively destroyed the intrinsic nature of learning. Education has become extrinsically driven and this has created major motivational problems in the classroom and workplace. This is as true for teachers and parents as it is for students. If you want to reward an aspect of learning then reinforce the effort, but treat equally and joyfully the appearance of failure and success.

Other enemies of education are the labelling of children as 'slow', 'weak', 'average' or 'brilliant', the confusion of intelligence with level of knowledge, lack of appreciation of all areas of knowledge, large class sizes, programme-centered rather than person-centered curricula, poor leadership and little back-up of psychological and social services.

## Q5. WHY DO SO MANY CHILDREN GO FOR THE AVERAGE IN SCHOOL?

Have you ever asked yourself the question: why do so many adults not go for promotion in their jobs, not pursue further courses of study, not seek out new friendships and relation- ships, not examine new philosophies and spiritualities, and go to the same place for their holidays every year? The most common answer to this question is that people prefer to play it safe and not risk failure, success or rejection. To delve into new thinking might demand change, which could trigger ridicule, failure and rejection and, finally, a new holiday destination carries so many unpredictabilities!

What has happened to the sense of adventure that you witness in infants and toddlers? How has it come about that children's natural curiosity and innate love of learning has become eroded? Furthermore, how can adults who go for the average be a source of inspiration to children?

Certainly, the greatest impediment to both children's and adults' progress in living is fear of failure, fear of success and fear of rejection.

One of the reasons why teaching has become such a stressful occupation is because some 70 to 80 per cent of students 'go for the average' and teachers, as well as hard-pressed parents, find it next to impossible to raise the academic sights of these young people. I meet many parents who are concerned about their son's or daughter's weak motivation to learn, but they meet with a brick wall when they attempt to raise the matter. The parents know that their children's academic achievements will play a significant role in determining their career choice and career path. These parents truly wonder why their offspring do not see the logic of their advice and take the necessary remedial action. However, emotion is always stronger than reason and there are not-so-apparent reasons why children choose the 50 per cent solution. What is startling about this solution is that it reduces the most common threats to children's need to feel accepted – failure, success and rejection. It does this by reducing the expectations of parents and teachers, and children subconsciously know that with a minimum of effort they can reach the average, thereby, paradoxically, eliminating failure, success and rejection in one ingenious stroke!

There are a number of possible reasons why children adopt the 50 per cent solution:

▫ Imitation of parents' and teachers' own 'average' defensive behaviour
▫ Unrealistic expectations by parents who are success and prestige addicted

▫ Comparison with a sibling who is highly academically achieving
▫ Punishment of what parents and teachers perceive as failure experiences
▫ Peer influence

Whatever the causes may be, it is equally important to examine the intentions of the defensive behaviour. Definitely going for the average does have the powerful results of controlling parents' and teachers' expectations, as well as reducing experiences of criticism, hurt and rejection.

If parents and teachers are to have any impact on this protective behaviour, they need to first look at their own approach to life, work and academic challenges. There is no point in parents and teachers asking children to do what they do not do themselves. Children are quick to see the presence of double standards and will resist change.

It is imperative that parents and teachers do not attack, criticise and condemn their children's reluctance to aim higher academically, as this will only serve to escalate the defensive reaction. After all, any attempt to take a weapon from an enemy will result in his holding onto it all the more or his grabbing another weapon. Labelling the young person as 'lazy', 'impossible' or 'loser', or threatening doom and gloom are not to be recommended. What is important is to understand the need for the 50 per cent solution and to target those behaviours and aspects of self that the child dare not show – for example, failure, success, high intelligence and love of learning. Parents would do well to talk about the value and endless learning opportunities that failure provides, the hollowness of success as a measure of self-worth, our limitless intelligence, the adventure of learning and, more importantly, to give expression to the child's specialness (with no strings attached).

## Q6. CHILDREN HAVE DIFFERENT LEARNING STYLES, DON'T THEY?

Each person tends to have a different style of dressing, walking, talking, relating, eating, etc. The purpose of these different 'styles' is an attempt by the child or adult to express their innate individuality and uniqueness. What has not often been appreciated by parents and teachers is that each child within a family tends to adopt a different learning style. Furthermore, another consideration that has been a serious omission in appreciating how learning occurs is that parents and teachers come to their task of teaching children with their own learning styles. When there is a mismatch between an adult's learning style and a particular child's learning style, then learning difficulties are likely to emerge for that child.

For too long the idea has prevailed that failure to under-stand and master a particular subject is due to a child not having the aptitude for the subject or that some children are just better able to learn than others and that some subjects are beyond certain children! For example, it was long thought that advanced mathematics, science and physics were beyond girls. That notion has been turned totally on its head: girls are now outdoing boys across all school subjects.

There needs to be recognition by parents and teachers of the limitless potential of each child, and an acknowledgement of the fact that children are eager and capable learners, provided they are given a safe and adventurous learning environment. Parents and teachers need to reflect on their own experiences of learning and try not to project their fears and doubts about their intelligence onto children. Children tend to be influenced more by the actions of adults than by their words. It is known that children as young as six or seven show fears around learning through picking up on the anxieties that parents and teachers show around learning and examinations. If parents and teachers want to positively influence a child's experience of learning and their progress in school – which will in turn influence their ability to take advantage of opportunities later in life – they must first free themselves of their own fears of failure or addiction to success. They need also to recover the adventure of learning and work.

What enormously helps a child's progress in the acquisition of knowledge and skills is the recognition that each child within a family ingeniously finds a way to be different in the way he or she learns. It is a truism that each child in a family goes the opposite way to the other and that each child has a different parent. To treat all the children the same means that the parent herself does not appreciate her own individuality and difference in how she operates in the world, and this blocks her from seeing the uniqueness of the child and the different ways he finds to manifest his uniqueness. Not only do children show different learning styles, they also show different learning preferences. A child who shows a weak knowledge of a particular subject is not 'slow' or 'weak' intellectually; it probably is the case that his preference, and therefore his motivation, lies elsewhere. Teachers, too, need to be aware of these phenomena when faced with a class of children. In the same way that each child has a different parent, so too each child has a different teacher. The teacher who fails to recognise the individuality and different learning styles and different learning preferences of his students piles up many difficulties for himself and for the children.

It is important that parents and teachers become familiar with different learning styles – visual, read-write, auditory and kinaesthetic. From an early age children express their difference in learning style. For example, some may naturally draw their ideas, while others may express an early interest in books; some may excitedly tell their ideas to others through language, while others may gravitate towards hands-on experience. Differences in learning styles and subject preferences among children do not reflect differences in learning ability or intelligence. Teachers and parents need to reflect on their own particular learning style and subject preference and be wary that a mismatch between their ways and the child's ways does not become a source of conflict. Acknowledgement and celebration of difference is the hallmark of a positive and dynamic learning environment.

## Q7. MY CHILD IS REFUSING TO GO TO SCHOOL BECAUSE HIS TEACHER SHOUTS. WHAT CAN I DO?

Over the years parents have brought me children complaining of abdominal pain, nausea and, sometimes, vomiting. Some of these children also exhibited temper tantrums and even banged their heads off doors. These symptoms occurred usually in the morning. Medical examination by family doctors revealed no organic bases to the abdominal pains. Attempts to force these children to go to school resulted in the escalation of these distressing symptoms.

When children are asked 'Why don't you want to go to school?' several answers emerge – not wanting to leave their mother; being bullied by other children; hating school; being shouted at by a teacher. The latter reason is common, and one child described it well to his mother when she enquired 'Why don't you want to go to school?' 'Cos teacher shouts'. The mother replied 'But love, I shout!' Wonderfully, the child responded 'But Mom, you shout gently'.

We have come to some level of maturity regarding the physical and sexual neglect of children, but the emotional hurting of children, which is far more frequent, intense and enduring, is not an issue to which we yet give serious consideration. Nonetheless, the effects of the emotional hurting of children are now well documented, and abdominal pain and aggressively acting out are some of its manifestations.

There is no intention to blame or criticise teachers. Indeed, when a teacher manifests the frequent, intense and enduring behaviour of shouting in class, that teacher needs help and support to resolve the difficulties underlying her difficult behaviour. Teachers I have helped with shouting in class have expressed underlying fears of not being in control, of criticism, of inadequacy and of how others see them.

It is a truism that the child's symptoms and the teacher's emotional hurting of children are cries for help. What is a parent to do when confronted with such a situation? Many parents find it very threatening to approach the class teacher about the shouting in the classroom. They are afraid of the teacher becoming defensive and the possibility that their child may be victimised or ignored in class. The temptation for some parents is to do nothing, or dilute what the child is saying or move the child to another school. The latter response needs to be a last, not a first resort.

When parents, because of their own fears, do not stand up for their child's right to physical, sexual, emotional, intellectual and social safety within the school and classroom, the child will feel hugely let down. The danger is that such a child will stop expressing how he feels and will not tell the parent about future experiences that are threatening to his welfare.

When a parent does not feel secure enough to positively confront a teacher on the threatening behaviour, it is crucial that she seeks support from the child's father or a good friend. When the two parents (or parent and friend) go to talk to the teacher, they need to go with the understanding that the teacher is not deliberately threatening the child, but nonetheless the shouting needs to stop. In as much as the child needs the parent's understanding, so does the teacher. Understanding a behaviour is not a means of diluting or excusing the behaviour. On the contrary, understanding involves the recognition of the effects of the threatening behaviour on the children and the determination that the threat has to be removed. However, understanding also involves looking at what causes the teacher to act in that way. The teacher's troubling behaviour is an opportunity for him or her to look into their own hearts and discover the sources of their shouting. It is incumbent on the school to provide all the help needed for this teacher, and this needs to include professional help when required.

When approaching the teacher on the difficult behaviour, it is best to invite the help of the teacher. Attack will definitely receive a defensive response and rightly so. Attack implies judgement and there is no surer action to trigger an attack back. An example of a mature approach would be 'Mr Murray, a difficulty has arisen with Michael (the child). He is experiencing abdominal pain and nausea and is even physically hurting himself because he is afraid of your shouting in the classroom. We need your support and help to make it safe for our child to return to school.'

My experience is, that nine times out of ten, a teacher will respond positively to such a request. A partnership between teacher and parent can then be arranged to create safety in the classroom for the child.

In the situation where a teacher becomes defensive, initially it is wise not to get into fighting with the teacher, but positively say 'I'm sure that on consideration you will help us on this matter'. Sometimes, following their defensive reaction, a teacher does find it in her heart to correct her behaviour or to get help if this proves difficult.

In a situation where no change occurs, the positive pursuance of the matter is vital. This may involve one or more of several actions: talking to the school principal, school manager, parent's association, school inspector, solicitor. Even if you have chosen to move your child to another school, pursuance of the issue to resolution is important for the other children and for the teacher.

## Q8. HOW CAN I HELP MY CHILD TO FEEL CONFIDENT IN SCHOOL?

Too often children are told they are 'stupid', 'slow', 'lazy', 'average', 'bright', 'very intelligent'. None of these labels is correct. Science has demonstrated that human beings use only 1 or 2 per cent of their brain cells and that they have limitless capability.

Parents, teachers and children tend to confuse knowledge with intelligence. Furthermore, there is no undisputed evidence that differences in intelligence are genetically determined. My own profession of psychology has done much to perpetuate that confusion by suggesting that so-called intelligence tests measure intelligence. Intelligence tests only measure knowledge, and only a limited range of knowledge at that. Indeed, research has shown that intelligence tests are very poor predictors of career development.

Differences emerging between children in their first days at school have to do with knowledge and skills and not with intelligence. Children come from different home and cultural backgrounds; some will have the benefit of having experienced one-to-one conversations with parents, of being read to frequently, of a stimulating home environment, of an emphasis on love of learning and so on. These children will show higher knowledge levels than children who have not had such experiences; but the difference lies in experience, not in capability. The confusion of certain types of knowledge with intelligence must stop. Typically, it is assumed that children who are good at reading and mathematics are clever and that those poor in those subjects have low intelligence.

Very often these latter children are sent for special needs education, which reinforces the 'slow' and 'dull' labels. These children always show knowledge in other areas, but the 'brightness' of this is rarely seen. If special needs teaching is going to continue to be an aspect of the school system, then it needs to be applied across the board of all knowledge areas, not just reading and mathematics.

The same holds true for streaming classes – otherwise these unfair practices will continue to discriminate against children who possess knowledge in non-academic areas. These interventions undermine children's beliefs about their intellectual potential and can cause major self-worth problems. The introduction of an academic and practical Leaving Certificate examination has gone further down the road in exacerbating such discriminatory practices.

I have worked with families where one child was regarded as a genius in school and the other needed special help. However, when it came to sports and making friends, the so-called 'weak' child could run rings around the so-called 'clever' child.

When children from sub-cultures – for example, travelling people – come into our schools they are far behind the other children in many of the curriculum subjects, but they would 'buy and sell' these children.

All children possess knowledge, and parents and educators need to step outside their blinkered value system to see and wonder at the different types of knowledge children bring to classrooms. Some children possess amazing knowledge and use of their bodies, others are ingenious at humour or can charm you up to your eyes. There are children who are masters at developing relationships and there are those whose emotional sensitivity to the moods of others are finely tuned.

It is indicative of bias that such children may be described as 'good with their feet', 'good with their hands', 'great mixers', 'sensitive', 'real jokers', but they are rarely described as intelligent. It is time to appreciate that children exhibit genius in all sorts of ways: wit, humour, sports, athletics, social skills, emotional sensitivity, art, mechanics, linguistics.

It is essential for each family member's total development that they are frequently reminded of their limitless capacity to learn and that mistakes and failures are treated simply as indicators of their present knowledge and skills level and as opportunities for further learning.

It is a sad reflection on our culture that only about 2 to 10 per cent of children and adults have any sense of their wondrous capability. What most of us experience is a deep lack of confidence and a belief that many challenges are beyond us. The frequent affirmation of each family member's limitless capability gives a powerful boost to the process of individuation and the attainment of knowledge; its absence can lead to avoidance of challenge, over-anxiety, perfectionism, 'playing it safe', rebelliousness or apathy. Any of these reactions slows down or completely blocks the development of the independence and individuality of each family member and their love of and excitement around acquiring knowledge.

## Q9. HOW CAN A PARENT NOT PASS ON HER OWN FEARS OF EXAMINATIONS TO HER CHILDREN?

Few parents and young people see examinations as a challenge, an adventure and an opportunity to communicate knowledge and skills learned. Regrettably, most face these tests with fear and trepidation. It certainly does not help young people when their parents, either verbally or non-verbally, communicate anxiety and pressure for high exam performance. Students are under enough pressure from an educational system that has lost sight of learning as an exciting challenge and has failed to develop a more effective and fair system of evaluating children's level of knowledge.

It is a fact that the present Leaving Certificate examination results determine whether or not entrance is gained to third-level education, while the government continues to fail to provide an adequate number of third-level places. This necessitates an unfair level of academic achievement and competitiveness. The unfairness of the points system does nothing to show young people they are members of a caring, just society.

Furthermore, the high points needed to gain places for certain highly regarded professional careers in no way guar-antees the best people for these professions. For example, members of the medical profession have the highest rate of suicide, drug and alcohol addiction, and marital and family breakdown. Schools and teachers also get entrapped by the examination system, and they are being pressurised by moves to evaluate schools on examination results.

Education is not just about the cognitive development of children: it is also about the physical, emotional, social, sexual, creative and spiritual growth of children. Bringing children to a place of peace and acceptance of themselves and others and encouraging their capacity to embrace the expansiveness of life is far more important than high examination results.

Teachers must resist all attempts at a narrow academic evaluation and put forward proposals for wider assessments. Accountability is integral to the practice of all professions, including parenting, but it must reflect all aspects and responsibilities of the profession.

Apart from acquainting students with the fact that they are victims of government failure, there are a number of vital messages that parents, teachers and politicians need to get across to students, so that at least some of the pressures of the unfair system are reduced:

- A student's worth is independent of an examination result.
- A successful examination result does not mean the student who is successful is deemed more worthy than the student who has not attained his or her ambition.
- Loving relationships are not threatened or determined by examination results.
- School examination results are not a measure of intelligence, but merely reflect a person's current levels of certain types of knowledge.
- School examinations fail to measure far more important areas of knowledge and skills, such as emotional, social, creative, spiritual, humorous, physical and sports abilities, life skills and streetwise behaviours.
- Success and failure are relative terms – and there is no such phenomenon as a success or failure of a person.

The central issue is that parents and teachers must not live their lives through their children's examination and other performances. Children need to be loved for themselves, not for what they do. Furthermore, failure and success are integral to progress in life, and to make fish of one and flesh of the other misses this fundamental principle of learning.

Learning is love made visible, and the tragedy is that it has become a misery and a threat for so many people. Failure and success rotate each other; failure sets the next learning target of a particular challenge and success sets the ground for a new challenge. Failure and success should never have been used as motivating forces; the result has been to dry up the love and eagerness to learn that is present in infants. The target of praise, encouragement and reward must be the sacred efforts to learn, never the performance. It is essential that adults correct these issues in their own lives before they can convince children of their authenticity.

The fact that examinations are not a measure of intelligence, but of knowledge, is rarely communicated to students. There is no such thing as a weak, slow, average or bright student. All students are geniuses.

The reality that they may not always express their intelligence in ways that fit in with the expectations of parents, teachers and society is no excuse for labelling children. It is reasonable to enquire of students why they are motivated towards or making progress in a particular school subject, but it is counterproductive to criticise them or assume that they are 'slow' or 'below average'. Children cleverly take on the labels that are put on them, and they use them to good effect to reduce further threats to the expression of their real selves.

## Q10. ANY IDEA WHY MY CHILD IS NOT THRIVING AT SCHOOL?

Mere physical presence does not in any way ensure learning. When children are not attentive, the concern is not their lack of attention but the need to discover why they are not present to the adventure of learning.

The prime need, not only of children but of all adults, is to love and be loved. The second most powerful need is to learn. Parents and teachers tend to see learning as what is done in the classroom and do not appreciate children's major learning adventures in emotionality, creativity, physicality, sensitivity, social ability, music, arts, sports, mechanics, play and spirituality.

Once a child is not thriving in the academic subjects, most parents react in ways that do not benefit their child's progress. They may show annoyance, aggression or over-anxiousness, all of which are guaranteed to exacerbate the situation. They may compare the child to a sibling or cousin or neighbour's offspring, but comparisons are acts of emotional rejection and will cause either withdrawal or temper outbursts. In a world of individuals it makes absolutely no sense to compare.

One thing that parents can be assured of is that their daughter or son has an innate urge to express his or her own uniqueness, individuality and difference. Indeed, within the family, each child will ingeniously find a way to express their individuality and it is not at all unusual to find that children go in the opposite direction to each other in emotional, social, physical and creative expression. Typically, within a family of four, you may have 'the academic', 'the carer', 'the charmer' and 'the athlete'.

It is wise for both parents and teachers to identify the unique ways in which each child expresses his or her innate difference and, most importantly, to affirm that wonderful process. This does not mean that you allow a child to slide out of responsibilities that subconsciously he does not see as part of his identity. But it does mean that approaching areas of poor attainment and low motivation is done with sensitivity to the child's unique expression of self. When a son or daughter is affirmed for his or her unique self-expression, and when encouragement and support are given to what are perceived by parents and teachers as the 'difficult areas', positive movement is likely to occur.

One of the assumptions that parents may make regarding their child's poor-to-average academic progress is that he or she is 'weak' intellectually and that there is no point in trying 'to make a silk purse out of a sow's ear'. This response undermines the confidence of the child, who has limitless ability to learn any field of knowledge. Lack of ability is not the issue, but rather lack of motivation. Sometimes the latter may arise from one child's determination not to compete with an older sibling who is always 'top of the class'. Other times it may be that the child is carrying deep emotional doubts about being loved and seen for self, and school learning is not a priority issue.

Other possibilities are peer pressure 'not to be smart', or bullying, or teachers who employ cynicism or sarcasm, or hidden abuses that the child is terrified of revealing. Only the individual boy or girl knows the true reasons for poor motivation and low attainment levels and only he or she can open the door to let you in to that inner world. They are unlikely to let you in if you come banging on the door, or are over-anxious or show little belief or compare him or her to others.

Patience, love, support, understanding and belief in children are what are needed for them to feel safe enough to bring us into their worlds. Parents also need to keep in mind that their responsibility is to support their children in their unique life journey and to let go of the notion that children are there to fulfil their (the parent's) projections.

## Q11. HOW CAN I BEST SUPPORT MY CHILD AROUND SCHOOL AND STATE EXAMINATIONS?

It is now commonly acknowledged that some parents put pressure on their children to achieve highly in examinations. This focus on exam performance starts in primary school and increases in tempo as children progress through secondary school, reaching a crescendo coming up to the Leaving Certificate.

What needs to be appreciated is the reasons why parents put such undue emphasis on their children's exam results. It is undoubtedly the case that all parents want the best for their children and that they want to be seen as caring and effective parents; some parents view their children's potential or poor academic performance as a reflection on their parenting.

In order to offset the judgement of others, they often pressurise their children to bring home the good school report card.

Parents who are vulnerable to the criticisms of others need understanding, support and help to free themselves of such dependencies; portraying them as 'bad' parents only confirms their worst fears and pushes them deeper into protecting themselves – with resultant increased expectations of their children.

There are other parents who have fears of academic or occupational or domestic or social failure, and they put huge pressures on themselves to succeed; this, in turn, is projected onto their offspring. These parents also need compassion and direction in order to come to a place where they no longer equate their unique worth with a transient success experience.

Parents and children alike need to embrace failure and success as integral to learning and not as an index of either their capability or lovability. Failure and success are the nuts and bolts of learning: without failure, no success; without success, no failure.

What counts mostly in learning is effort. Once this is nurtured, encouraged, praised and rewarded, adults and children will thrive educationally and occupationally.

While it is true that parents need to resolve their own emotional problems and not project these on to each other or their children, it is equally true to say that there have not been too many emotionally safe forums for adults to accomplish such maturity.

In the same way that judgements, criticism, ridicule, cynicism, sarcasm and irritability undermine children's security, similar reactions to parents further undermine their security. Schools and communities could be venues where courses for parents on self-development, parenting and educating their children could be organised. For those parents in need of more in-depth help, a community-based and paid confidential counselling service is required.

During the process of redeeming their own self-worth and independence, and coming up to exam time, parents can do much to help themselves and their children to cope with examination stress.

▢ Acknowledge to themselves and to their children their own fears of failure and worries about what others think of them. Such openness makes it safe for children to voice anxieties; it equalises the relationship between parents and children and it sets the foundation for both to see that their worth lies in themselves and not in examination results.

▢ Stay largely on the sidelines of young people's preparation and study for examinations and, from there, encourage, support and acknowledge the efforts being made. It would show caring also to ask is there anything they can do to make it easier.

□ Avoid criticism, cajoling, ridicule, irritability and aggression as means of motivating children to study. Such responses serve only to decrease motivation.

□ When minimal (or no) study efforts are being made, express concern and enquire as to who and what is causing such apathy. These questions need to be expressed in a loving way; any show of hostility and the young person will quickly withdraw or react aggressively. It is also true to say that any show of undue anxiety on the face of parents may catapult children into overworking or rebelling.

□ When children are making excessive efforts to learn and manifesting anxiety about results, it is vital that parents reassure them that they are loved for themselves and that no matter what result they get, it will neither add nor detract from that love. Parents also need to encourage these children to lower their expectations of themselves, set more realistic goals and study at a less intense level.

□ Do not use material goods (new outfit, motorbike, car, holiday) as a means of increasing motivation and application to study. Children see very clearly the manipulation aspect of this ploy and will see that parents are more concerned about their own image rather than their child's welfare.

□ Finally, humour is a great means of keeping our feet on the ground and not losing sight of what counts between parents and children – love.

## Q12. HOW CAN I TAKE THE STING OUT OF SCHOOL HOMEWORK FOR MY CHILD?

The key to helping children with homework is for parents to be aware of the influence of self-esteem on their children's educational progress and to ensure that all helping inter-actions with children are ones that elevate their self-esteem.

Another critical factor is ensuring at all times that children experience only positive associations with homework. This involves making sure that every effort is seen as an attain-ment, and that mistakes and failures are seen purely as further opportunities for learning. This puts the emphasis constantly on effort and not on performance. Remaining calm and encouraging when children experience learning difficulties is also important.

At the same time, parents must not allow children to slide out of educational responsibilities, though they must avoid getting trapped into conflict with them. Maintaining empathic interest in their educational growth guarantees children's commitment to learning. Too many parents let children get on with the business of schooling and forget that children need their parents to notice what they do on an everyday basis. Absence of parental interest in children's learning frequently leads to apathy and loss of motivation to learn.

Setting up fixed study areas in the home is a further important factor. You need to be sure that such areas are as free of distraction as possible and in no way near the television or other sources of entertainment. When studying, it is also best that children are separated from each other. Be sure to visit the children during their study times and offer help, support, encouragement and 'treats'.

If asked for help try to avoid the temptation to do things for your children; good teaching means aiding and guiding children in a step-by-step way to do things for themselves. Doing things for them deprives children of learning to do things for themselves and keeps them helpless.

You need to be firm with your children from an early age with regard to being orderly and tidy, as these behaviours will transfer to their school responsibilities. Do not accept sloppy or careless work from children. Let them know firmly and calmly that acceptance of such irresponsible efforts would mean not loving them and not caring for their future.

After all, an acceptance of such sloppy work implies that you (as the parent) are not loving or respecting them fully or properly as a unique person with limitless potential.

Parents need to help their children cope with the frustration that can arise when things go wrong, or when they have difficulty in grasping a concept. If your child is feeling frustrated, help him or her to let go of the task for a while, do something calming (for example, go to the kitchen and have a soft drink or do a relaxation exercise) and then get the child to complete some other learning task that has been assigned. After the latter is completed, encourage and support the child to return to the earlier frustrating activity and help and guide him or her through the learning task.

A sense of humour lightens the whole process and also keeps the child more in touch with reality. The essential learning experience for the child is to realise that tension, frustration, anxiety and temper block the learning process and it is useless to continue until they have become calm and relaxed again.

Homework can be a major source of conflict between parents and children. The amount of homework assigned to children needs to be carefully monitored. A general guideline is that from ages five to eight children should only get a maximum of one hour's homework, from eight to fifteen years two hours should be the maximum and from fifteen to eighteen years three hours should be the maximum.

Some children may of course dilly-dally when doing homework and then complain about the amount of time it takes. When in doubt, check with the child's teacher how long homework should take. Teachers need to estimate homework time according to the learning rate of the majority of the class rather than the rate of those who learn more quickly.

When children are doing their homework, let them know that help is available and be sure to look in on them, giving words of praise and encouragement and perhaps a 'treat'. When homework is completed, it is important that one of the parents checks the child's efforts, praises the attainment achieved and points out where the next effort needs to be focused.

Where there has been genuine and sincere effort, even though the child may have got something wrong, put the emphasis on what he or she has attained and let the teacher shape up the next effort needed within the classroom.

Do not get a child to repeat homework just because some mistake has been made. This is very punishing for children and homework now begins to have negative associations. It is, of course, a different situation if mistakes occur because the effort was rushed, careless and slipshod.

Finally, following homework, the best reward is always affirmation and praise but children may also be rewarded with a favoured activity. This practice leads to children having positive associations with homework.

In carrying out the above suggestions regarding homework it is important that predictability and consistency are maintained. If a parent or other childminder cannot be patient and calm with children's homework efforts and the mistakes they make, it is best that that person is not involved in helping with homework.

Where children are consistently attempting to avoid home-work and studying or are over-diligent and even scrupulous, these need to be recognised as signs of avoidance and perfectionism and as revelations of self-esteem difficulties. Attention to the child's self-esteem is then a priority.

## Q13. HOW CAN I HELP MY CHILD WHO IS TIMID AND FEARFUL?

Over the years many parents have complained to me of their children requiring special needs education, sometimes even within the first year of attending school. Very often these children come from advantaged homes, where both parents have professional careers and believe in and strongly endorse the educational development of themselves and their children. These parents often follow up their complaints regarding their children's 'slowness' with 'and you know he's very fearful and timid'. From that observation I gain an insight into the possible causes for these particular children's difficulties in learning. I enquire of the parents of how they responded to the child when she was doing her school homework, or, indeed, learning any new task. Frequently, the response I get is that they shout, roar, hit, criticise, frown, show disappointment and are extremely pushy when teaching the child. When parents themselves dread mistakes and failures and are very conscious of how others view them, they are equally critical and punishing of themselves in their daily work and in their domestic and social lives. These parents do not see their children as separate from but as an extension of themselves, and any failure on the child's part is seen as a failure on their part. Hence the pressure they put on themselves not to fail is now extended to their child's behaviour, particularly the child's academic performance. The classic example of this phenomenon is the parent who is perfectionistic. Everything is spotlessly clean and perfectly placed in the home – what is displaced are children and/or partner. Some spouses have said to me 'how things are placed is more important than me or the children'. Perfectionism is an attempt to eliminate failure and, thereby, criticism and rejection. The effects of this on marriages and children's development can be devastating.

When parents are intolerant and hostile to children's mistakes, failures and rate of learning, these responses are absolutely terrifying for children. The prime need of children is to be loved. When love is withdrawn regularly through harshness, irritability, ridicule, disapproval, silent treatment and scoldings in response to mistakes, then children wisely develop ways to reduce the possibility of further hurt, humiliation and loss of love. The threat in this case is failure and one of the strongest protectors against failure is avoidance. With no effort there is no failure, and with no failure there is no criticism and rejection. It is just not safe for these children to take on the challenges of learning, and they intelligently 'drop out' of academic efforts. They often develop other protectors, the most common and most powerful being fear and timidity. Fear and timidity are strengths that children employ to get their parents (and sometimes teachers) to treat them more gently. After all, how do you approach a child or adult who is shy, timid and fearful? With caution, kid gloves, gently! Who is controlling whom? And you think of your child as intellectually slow? Hardly! However, until it becomes emotionally safe for these children to fail, to make mistakes and to struggle with learning some concepts and skills, they will cleverly and necessarily hold on to the protective strategies of avoidance, fear and timidity. These protectors are often maintained through childhood and into adulthood.

There are men and women I work with who come for help because they are taunted by others, including members of their family of origin, for being over-cautious, timid and fearful. When I tell them that these behaviours are strengths, not weaknesses, they stare at me with sceptical eyes. However, when I explore in what ways one or both parents responded to their learning efforts and failures, the response I get is 'oh my father (or mother) was hypercritical and sometimes physically violent'. I point out to them how ingenious they were when children to become over-cautious, fearful and timid. In becoming over-cautious, in doing things more slowly and carefully, you reduce the possibilities of making mistakes and thereby offset rejection. In becoming fearful and timid you reduce the intensity of the rejection experiences. I am very clear with these persons that I do not want them to let go of these protectors until they have come to a sense of their own goodness, uniqueness and worth and until they become both independent of failure and success and of how others view them.

All children's fears act as protectors. When children show fear of failure they are subconsciously driven into over-working or avoidance in order to avoid failure and consequent rejection. The fear of failure also has the protective function of attempting to reduce parents' and teachers' unrealistic expectations. However, fears in children have another wise function and that is to alert parents, teachers and other significant adults in the children's lives to wake up to the threats that are posed and to heal the insecurity by loving the children for themselves, not for what they do.

Other typical fears children manifest are fear of change, fear of taking on a new challenge, fear of meeting adults known to the parents, fear of the dark, fear of being left alone, fear of being bullied, fear of teachers and fear of not being liked.

Ask yourself what is the protective function of each of these fears and what are the fears attempting to alert you to? Each fear will tend to mean something different for each child. You would be surprised when you talk kindly to children about their fears how they will let you know the threats to their security that are operating and the means they use to reduce these threats. Be patient – children will only talk openly about their fears when they are sure your love for them will not be withdrawn when you hear or witness behaviours that do not measure up to your expectations of yourself and of them.

## Q14. HOW DOES THE FAMILY INFLUENCE CHILDREN'S LEARNING?

The most powerful culture that influences all our lives is the family culture. Every family is a unique culture, and members of this culture will apply their intellectual potential to acquire knowledge and skills that will help them to adapt to and develop in that social system. Children are not passive recipients of family influences. On the contrary, each child within a family strives actively to establish his or her own identity and will often go directly opposite to a brother or sister in his emotions, behaviour, creativity and intellect. This process of individuation continues when children move into the wider social systems of school, neighbourhood, peer group and so on. Owing to this process of identity formation, children will necessarily and creatively acquire knowledge in different areas of intellectual functioning, depending on what is valued and modelled by parents and significant others and how they can best be seen for themselves within the family and other social systems.

When children come from an 'advantaged' home, where mother and father have a close emotional relationship, where they have talked and read on a one-to-one basis to the child, where the parents themselves value and are actively involved in promoting their own learning, where strong educational stimulation of an academic nature is present, then their children will emerge from that home with high verbal and numerical knowledge, high general knowledge, good social and emotional skills, good physical co-ordination abilities and self-reliant and independent living skills. They will also possess a high to moderate level of self-worth, be motivated to learn and have a love of challenge.

When children come from a family culture wherein parents do not have a close emotional bond, where little one-to-one talking and reading has been done with the children, where education and academic learning has been neither modelled in or valued, these children will come into school classrooms with poor self-worth, poor linguistic and numerical skills, poor social and emotional knowledge and poor motivation to learn school knowledge. However, they may possess knowledge not appreciated or even seen by teachers – to mention a few: humour, sports skills, interpersonal knowledge (albeit of a defensive nature that controls, dominates and manipulates others) and manual skills. Frequently, these children are labelled 'slow' or 'weak' and would perform poorly in an intelligence test. *But they do not lack intelligence.* Certainly, they may have a weak knowledge of many of the school curriculum subjects and of the types of knowledge measured by an intelligence test, but they have *ingeniously* learnt what was necessary for them to survive within their unique family culture.

Problems in learning may also arise in families that may be materially and educationally 'advantaged' but which put major emphasis on academic performance and 'family image'. Children quickly learn, even at pre-school age, to adapt to such conditionality, or they rebel or develop clever avoidance and sickness strategies to offset emotional rejection. I have no doubt that parents always want the best for their children, but it is only possible to do this when parents are free of or at least know their own fears and complexes.

Each family is a unique culture and it is important that parents, who are the architects of that culture, evaluate how members interact with each other and how each feels about self. It is equally true that each school and each classroom is a unique culture and that parents need to be vigilant for any signs that their children are not thriving emotionally, socially and educationally within those different settings. Close liaison with the school and teachers is essential.

Children are born with a natural curiosity and eagerness to learn. To ensure that children do not lose the innate love of learning, parents would do well to take note of the following suggestions:

- Learning must never jeopardise parents' loving of children.
- Learning must only have positive associations.
- An absence of criticism, ridicule, cajoling or comparisons is crucial.
- Emphasis must be put on effort and not on performance.
- Failure must be embraced as an opportunity for further learning, not for criticism.
- Children must be seen for themselves, not for their academic attainments.
- Do not label children as 'weak', 'slow', 'brilliant'.
- Affirm each child for his or her unique and limitless intelligence.
- If you cannot be patient, do not help with homework.
- The presence of encouragement, support, belief in and fun eases the challenge of learning.

# INDEX